FLOWERS AND FAIRIES

After dancing in the sky, the fairies rest on Crystal Mountain.
Dragonfly, butterfly and ladybug take a nap.

INSTRUCTIONS ON PAGE 2

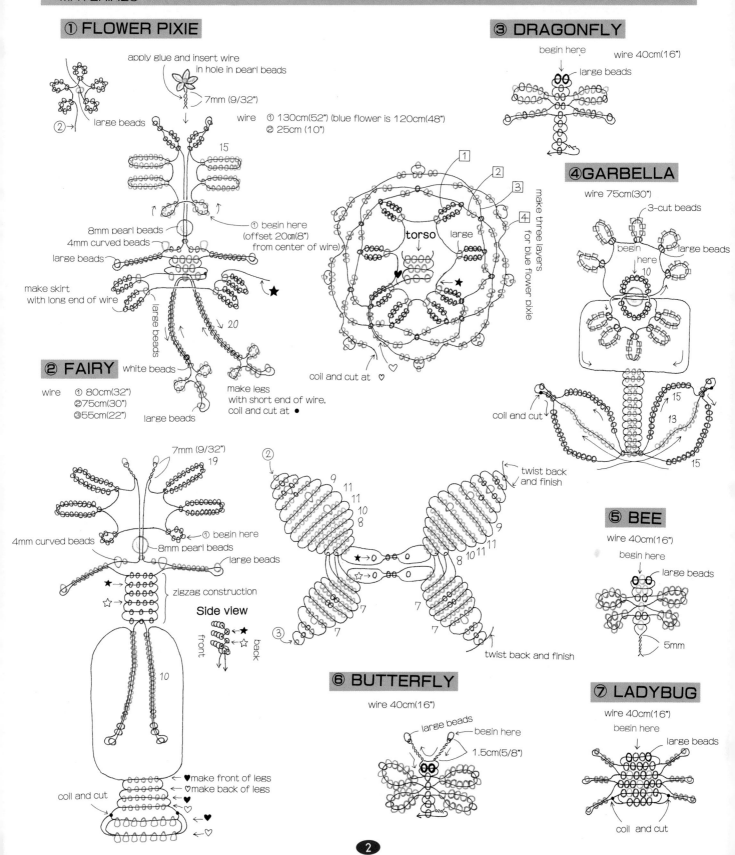

INSTRUCTIONS AND MATERIALS

small & large round beads, 3mm & 4mm curved beads, 3-cut beads, 5mm, 8mm & 10mm pearl beads, 4mmx8mm teardrop pearl beads, #34 wire, glue.

Use small round beads unless otherwise indicated

① FLOWER PIXIE

apply glue and insert wire in hole in pearl beads

7mm (9/32")

②→ large beads

wire ① 130cm(52") (blue flower is 120cm(48")
② 25cm (10")

15

① begin here
(offset 20cm(8")
from center of wire)

8mm pearl beads
4mm curved beads
large beads

make skirt
with long end of wire

large beads

20

② FAIRY

white beads

wire ① 80cm(32")
② 75cm(30")
③ 55cm(22")

large beads

make legs
with short end of wire,
coil and cut at ●

torso   large

coil and cut at ♡

make three layers
for blue flower pixie

③ DRAGONFLY

begin here

wire 40cm(16")

large beads

④ GARBELLA

wire 75cm(30")

3-cut beads

begin here   large beads

10

coil and cut

15
13
15

7mm (9/32")
19

4mm curved beads
8mm pearl beads
① begin here
large beads

zigzag construction

Side view

★ front
☆ back

②

9
11
11
10
8

twist back
and finish

★ ○
☆ ○

9
8 10 11
11

③→

7
7
7
7

twist back and finish

10

♥make front of legs
♡make back of legs

coil and cut

♥
♥
♥

⑤ BEE

wire 40cm(16")

begin here

large beads

5mm

⑥ BUTTERFLY

wire 40cm(16")

large beads   begin here

1.5cm(5/8")

⑦ LADYBUG

wire 40cm(16")

begin here

large beads

coil and cut

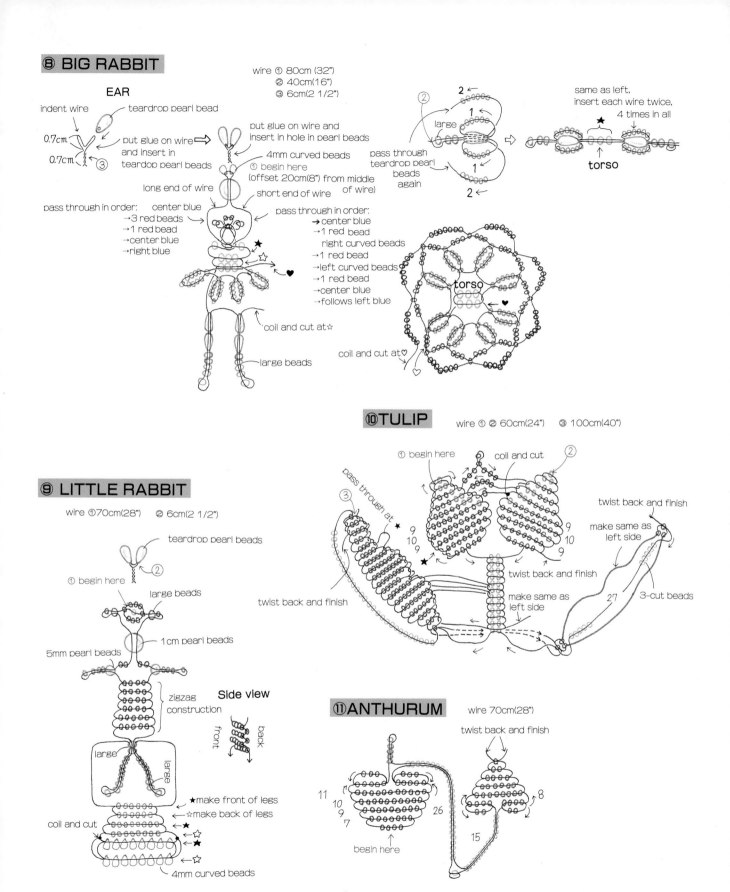

⑧ BIG RABBIT

wire ① 80cm (32")
② 40cm(16")
③ 6cm(2 1/2")

EAR

indent wire
teardrop pearl bead
0.7cm
0.7cm ③
put glue on wire and insert in teardrop pearl beads

put glue on wire and insert in hole in pearl beads

4mm curved beads
① begin here (offset 20cm(8") from middle of wire)

long end of wire
short end of wire

pass through in order:
center blue
→3 red beads
→1 red bead
→center blue
→right blue

pass through in order:
→center blue
→1 red bead
right curved beads
→1 red bead
→left curved beads
→1 red bead
→center blue
→follows left blue

coil and cut at ☆

large beads

②
2
large
1
1
2
2
pass through teardrop pearl beads again

★
same as left.
insert each wire twice.
4 times in all
torso

torso
♥
coil and cut at ♥
♥

⑨ LITTLE RABBIT

wire ①70cm(28")   ② 6cm(2 1/2")

teardrop pearl beads
②
① begin here

large beads
1cm pearl beads
5mm pearl beads

zigzag construction

Side view
front
back

large
large

★make front of legs
☆make back of legs

coil and cut
←★
←☆
←★
←☆

4mm curved beads

⑩ TULIP

wire ① ② 60cm(24")   ③ 100cm(40")

① begin here
coil and cut
②
③ pass through at ★

9
10 9
9

★
twist back and finish

9
10
9

make same as left side

twist back and finish

twist back and finish
make same as left side

27
3-cut beads

⑪ ANTHURUM

wire 70cm(28")

twist back and finish

11
10
9
7
26
15
8

begin here

3

THE WIZARD OF OZ

After the tornado carried her to Oz,
Dorothy and her three friends met the wizard and began their adventure

small & large round beads, 3mm square beads, 3 & 4mm curved beads, 3mm bugle beads, 3, 4, 5 & 8mm pearl beads, 4x8 & 5x7 oval pearl beads, #34 wire, glue.
Use large round beads unless otherwise indicated

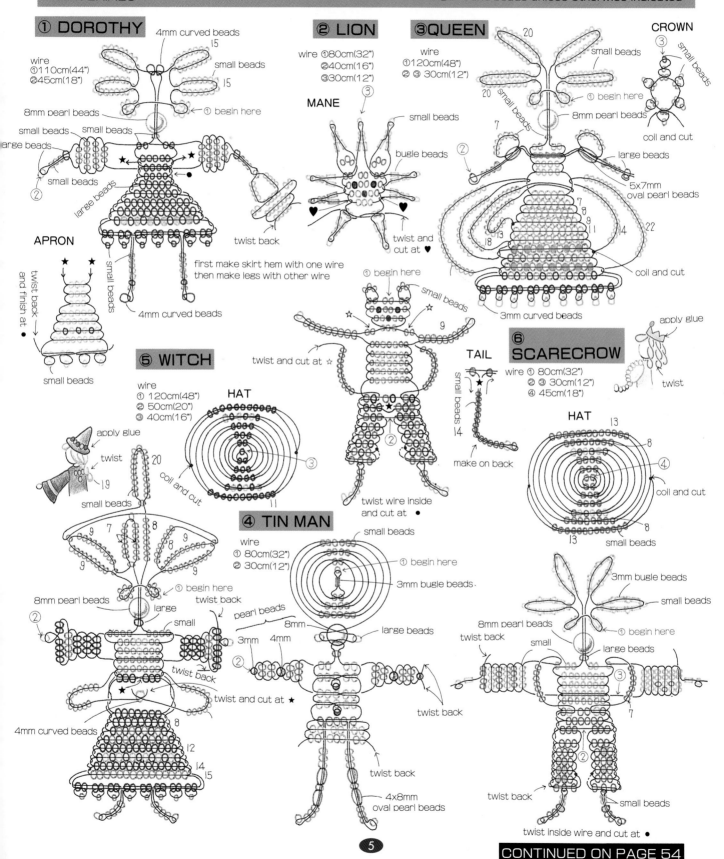

CONTINUED ON PAGE 54

ANNE'S ROOM

Let's make a house and all the furniture like chairs, table, bed and rocking chair!

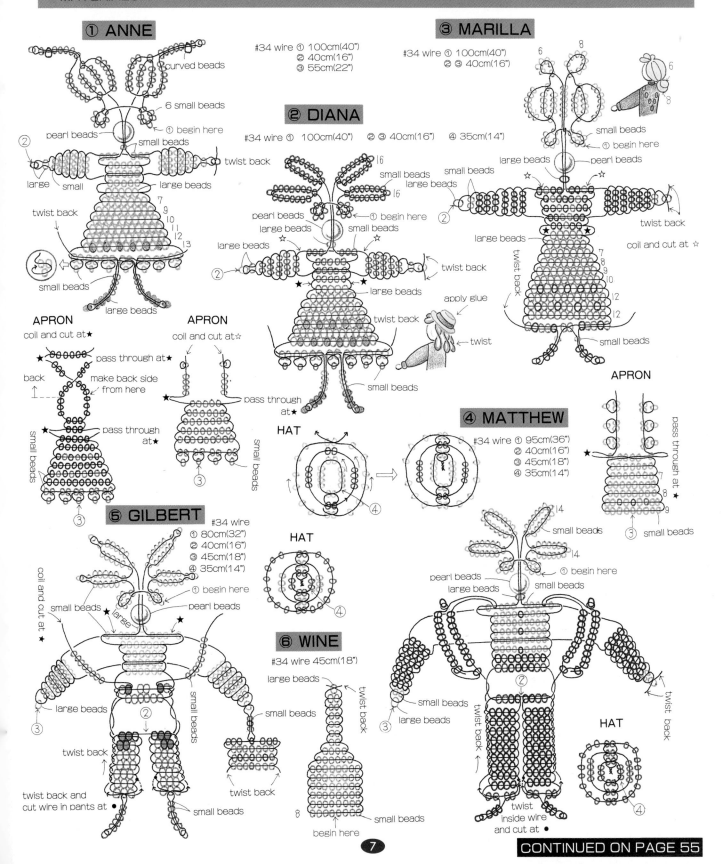

INSTRUCTIONS AND MATERIALS

small & large round beads. 3mm curved beads. 3-cut beads. 8mm pearl beads. # 30 & 34 wire. glue.

Use large round beads unless otherwise indicated

① ANNE

curved beads
6 small beads
pearl beads
① begin here
small beads
twist back
large   small
large beads
twist back
7
9
10
11
12
13
small beads
large beads

#34 wire ① 100cm(40")
         ② 40cm(16")
         ③ 55cm(22")

APRON
coil and cut at ★
back
pass through at ★
make back side from here
pass through at ★
small beads
③

APRON
coil and cut at ☆
pass through at ★
small beads
③

② DIANA

#34 wire ① 100cm(40") ② ③ 40cm(16") ④ 35cm(14")

16
small beads
large beads
16
pearl beads
① begin here
large beads   small beads
☆   ☆
large beads
②
twist back
★
large beads
twist back
apply glue
twist
small beads

HAT
④

③ MARILLA

#34 wire ① 100cm(40")
         ② ③ 40cm(16")

6   8
small beads
① begin here
large beads   pearl beads
☆   ☆
②
twist back
large beads
★   ★
coil and cut at ☆
twist back
7
8
9
10
12
12
small beads

6
8
small beads
8

APRON
pass through at ★
7
8
9
③ small beads

④ MATTHEW

#34 wire ① 95cm(36")
         ② 40cm(16")
         ③ 45cm(18")
         ④ 35cm(14")

14
small beads
① begin here
pearl beads
large beads   small beads
②
14
twist back
twist back
small beads
large beads
③
twist inside wire and cut at •

HAT
④

⑤ GILBERT

#34 wire
① 80cm(32")
② 40cm(16")
③ 45cm(18")
④ 35cm(14")

① begin here
coil and cut at ★
small beads
large
pearl beads
★
large beads
③
②
small beads
twist back
twist back and cut wire in pants at •
small beads

HAT
④

⑥ WINE

#34 wire 45cm(18")

large beads
twist back
small beads
small beads
③   large beads
twist back
8
begin here
small beads

CONTINUED ON PAGE 55

FOREST SYMPHONY

It's the Forest Symphony! Everyone's singing and dancing to the music of the animals.

small & large round beads, 3 & 4mm curved beads, 3-cut beads, 5mm pearl beads, #34 wire, glue.

Use small round beads unless otherwise indicated

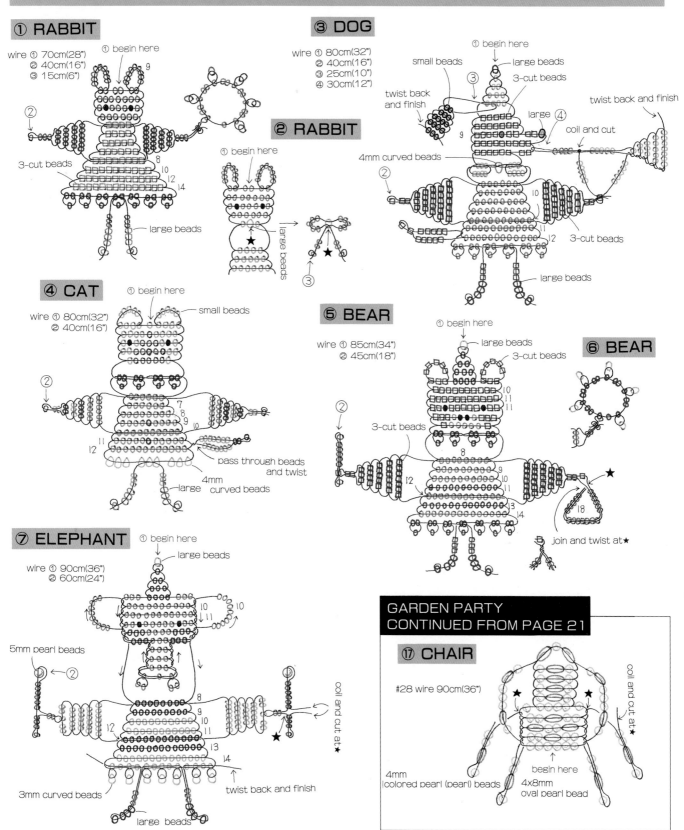

① RABBIT

wire ① 70cm(28")
　　② 40cm(16")
　　③ 15cm(6")

① begin here

9

②

3-cut beads

8

10

12

14

large beads

③ DOG

wire ① 80cm(32")
　　② 40cm(16")
　　③ 25cm(10")
　　④ 30cm(12")

① begin here

small beads

large beads

3-cut beads

③

twist back and finish

twist back and finish

9

large ④

coil and cut

②

4mm curved beads

10

11

12

3-cut beads

large beads

② RABBIT

① begin here

★

large beads

★

③

④ CAT

① begin here

small beads

wire ① 80cm(32")
　　② 40cm(16")

②

7

8

9

10

11

12

pass through beads and twist

4mm curved beads

large beads

⑤ BEAR

① begin here

large beads

3-cut beads

wire ① 85cm(34")
　　② 45cm(18")

②

3-cut beads

10

11

8

9

10

11

12

13

14

★

18

join and twist at ★

⑥ BEAR

⑦ ELEPHANT

① begin here

large beads

wire ① 90cm(36")
　　② 60cm(24")

10

11

10

11

5mm pearl beads

②

①

8

9

10

11

12

13

14

★

coil and cut at ★

3mm curved beads

large beads

twist back and finish

GARDEN PARTY CONTINUED FROM PAGE 21

⑰ CHAIR

#28 wire 90cm(36")

★

★

coil and cut at ★

4mm
(colored pearl (pearl) beads

begin here

4x8mm
oval pearl bead

THE CIRCUS COMES TO TOWN!

Clowns and a bear cub on a bike teeter on the highwire while other performers cavort below.

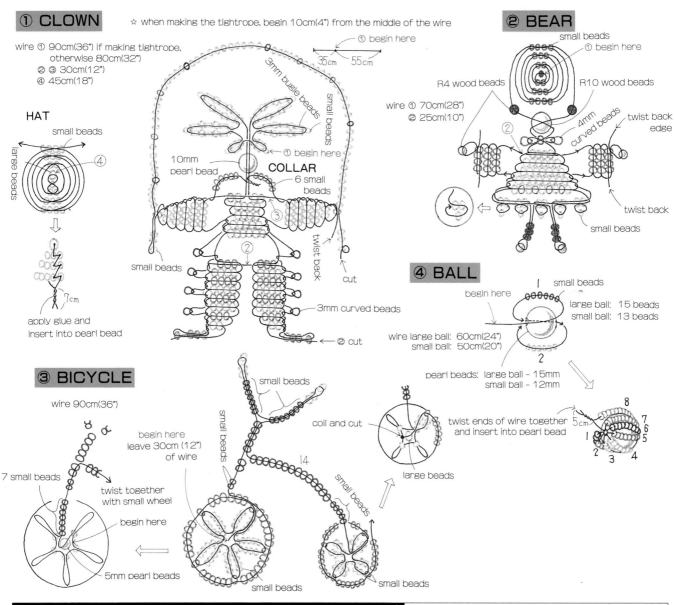

① CLOWN

☆ when making the tightrope, begin 10cm(4") from the middle of the wire

wire ① 90cm(36") if making tightrope,
otherwise 80cm(32")
② ③ 30cm(12")
④ 45cm(18")

① begin here

35cm 55cm

3mm bugle beads

small beads

HAT

small beads

large beads

④

apply glue and
insert into pearl bead

7cm

① begin here

10mm pearl bead

COLLAR
6 small beads

③

②

twist back

cut

small beads

3mm curved beads

② cut

② BEAR

small beads

① begin here

R4 wood beads

R10 wood beads

wire ① 70cm(28")
② 25cm(10")

②

4mm curved beads

twist back edge

twist back

small beads

④ BALL

begin here

small beads

large ball: 15 beads
small ball: 13 beads

wire large ball: 60cm(24")
small ball: 50cm(20")

pearl beads: large ball – 15mm
small ball – 12mm

2

twist ends of wire together
and insert into pearl bead

5cm

8
7
6
5
1
2
3
4

③ BICYCLE

wire 90cm(36")

small beads

begin here
leave 30cm (12")
of wire

7 small beads

twist together
with small wheel

begin here

5mm pearl beads

small beads

14

coil and cut

large beads

small beads

small beads

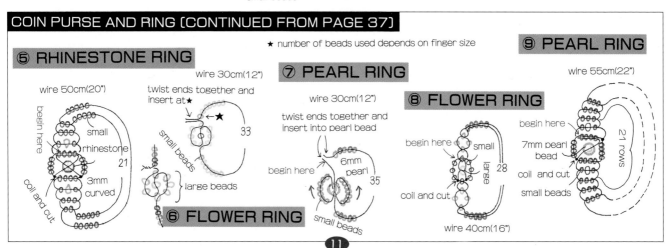

COIN PURSE AND RING [CONTINUED FROM PAGE 37]

★ number of beads used depends on finger size

⑤ RHINESTONE RING

wire 50cm(20")

begin here

small rhinestone

coil and cut

3mm curved

wire 30cm(12")

twist ends together and
insert at ★

small beads

large beads

33

⑨ PEARL RING

wire 55cm(22")

begin here

7mm pearl bead

coil and cut

small beads

21 rows

⑦ PEARL RING

wire 30cm(12")

twist ends together and
insert into pearl bead

begin here

6mm pearl

begin here

small beads

35

⑧ FLOWER RING

begin here

small

large

coil and cut

28

wire 40cm(16")

⑥ FLOWER RING

NEW YEAR'S

Children in traditional costume enjoy festive Japanese New Year's games.

GIRL'S BACK VIEW

INSTRUCTIONS AND MATERIALS

small & large round beads, 3 & 4mm curved beads, 3-cut beads 5 & 10mm pearl beads, #34 wire, glue.

Use large round beads unless otherwise indicated

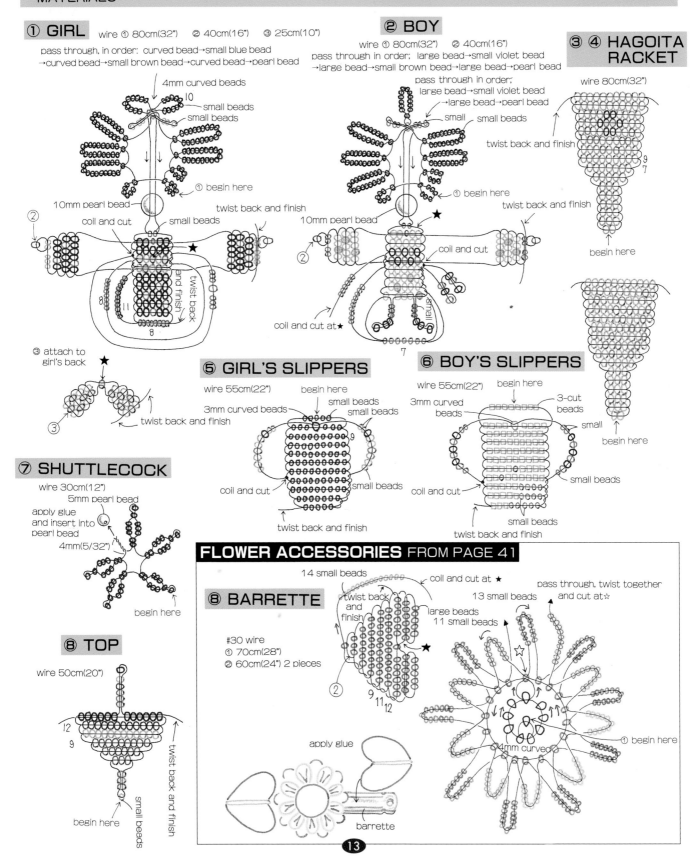

① GIRL

wire ① 80cm(32") ② 40cm(16") ③ 25cm(10")

pass through, in order: curved bead→small blue bead →curved bead→small brown bead→curved bead→pearl bead

4mm curved beads

10

small beads

small beads

① begin here

10mm pearl bead

coil and cut

small beads

twist back and finish

twist back and finish

8

11

8

② ② ★

③ attach to girl's back ★

③

twist back and finish

② BOY

wire ① 80cm(32") ② 40cm(16")

pass through in order; large bead→small violet bead →large bead→small brown bead→large bead→pearl bead

pass through in order; large bead→small violet bead →large bead→pearl bead

small small beads

① begin here

twist back and finish

10mm pearl bead

coil and cut

small

coil and cut at ★

②

7

③ ④ HAGOITA RACKET

wire 80cm(32")

twist back and finish

9 7

begin here

begin here

⑤ GIRL'S SLIPPERS

wire 55cm(22")

begin here

3mm curved beads

small beads

small beads

9

coil and cut

small beads

twist back and finish

⑥ BOY'S SLIPPERS

wire 55cm(22")

begin here

3mm curved beads

3-cut beads

small

coil and cut

small beads

small beads

twist back and finish

⑦ SHUTTLECOCK

wire 30cm(12")

5mm pearl bead

apply glue and insert into pearl bead

4mm(5/32")

begin here

⑧ TOP

wire 50cm(20")

12

9

twist back and finish

small beads

begin here

FLOWER ACCESSORIES FROM PAGE 41

14 small beads

coil and cut at ★

pass through, twist together and cut at ☆

13 small beads

⑧ BARRETTE

#30 wire
① 70cm(28")
② 60cm(24") 2 pieces

twist back and finish

large beads

11 small beads

★

②

9 11 12

apply glue

barrette

☆

① begin here

4mm curved

The base of dried clay covered with beads makes this doll set very stable.

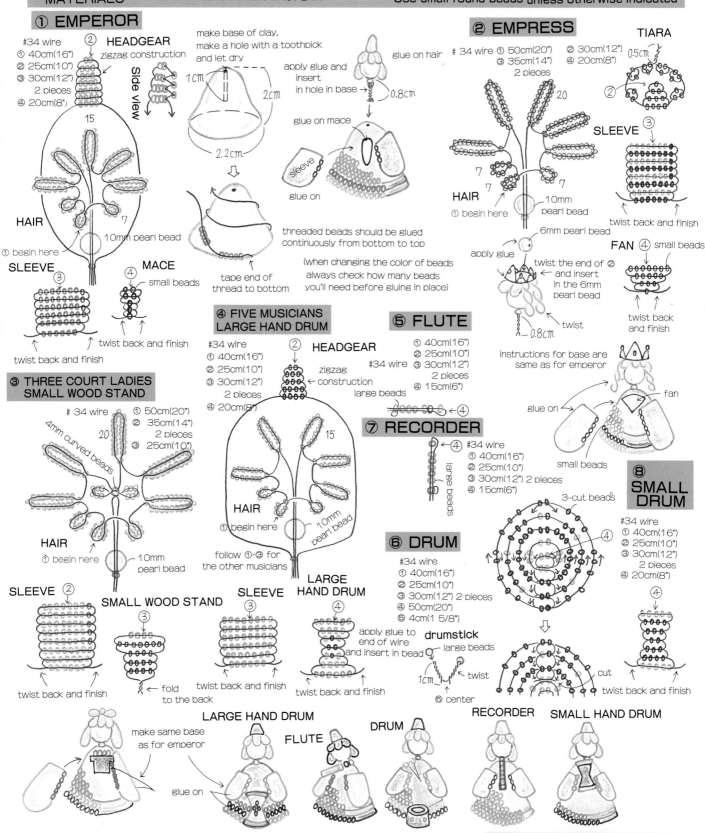

INSTRUCTIONS AND MATERIALS

small & large round beads, 4mm curved beads, small hexagonal beads, bugle beads, small beads, 6, 10 & 14mm pearl beads, 6x8mm oval pearl beads, #28 &34 wire, #20 craft thread, clay, glue.   **Use small round beads unless otherwise indicated**

① EMPEROR

#34 wire
① 40cm(16")
② 25cm(10")
③ 30cm(12") 2 pieces
④ 20cm(8")

HEADGEAR
zigzag construction

Side view

15

HAIR
① begin here

7

10mm pearl bead

SLEEVE
③

MACE
④ small beads

twist back and finish

twist back and finish

make base of clay, make a hole with a toothpick and let dry

1cm   2cm

2.2cm

apply glue and insert in hole in base

glue on hair

0.8cm

glue on mace

sleeve

glue on

threaded beads should be glued continuously from bottom to top

(when changing the color of beads always check how many beads you'll need before gluing in place)

tape end of thread to bottom

③ THREE COURT LADIES SMALL WOOD STAND

34 wire
① 50cm(20")
② 35cm(14") 2 pieces
③ 25cm(10")

4mm curved beads

20

HAIR
① begin here

10mm pearl bead

SLEEVE ②

SMALL WOOD STAND
③
fold to the back

SLEEVE ③

twist back and finish

④ FIVE MUSICIANS LARGE HAND DRUM

#34 wire
① 40cm(16")
② 25cm(10")
③ 30cm(12") 2 pieces
④ 20cm(8")

HEADGEAR
zigzag construction
large beads

②

15

HAIR
① begin here

10mm pearl bead

follow ①-③ for the other musicians

LARGE HAND DRUM
④

twist back and finish

② EMPRESS

34 wire
① 50cm(20")   ② 30cm(12")
③ 35cm(14")   ④ 20cm(8")
2 pieces

TIARA
0.5cm
②

SLEEVE ③

twist back and finish

20

7   7   7

HAIR
① begin here

10mm pearl bead

6mm pearl bead

apply glue

twist the end of ② and insert in the 6mm pearl bead

twist

0.8cm

FAN ④ small beads

twist back and finish

instructions for base are same as for emperor

glue on

fan

small beads

⑤ FLUTE

① 40cm(16")
② 25cm(10")
#34 wire ③ 30cm(12") 2 pieces
④ 15cm(6")

large beads ④

⑦ RECORDER

④
#34 wire
① 40cm(16")
② 25cm(10")
③ 30cm(12") 2 pieces
④ 15cm(6")

large beads

⑥ DRUM

#34 wire
① 40cm(16")
② 25cm(10")
③ 30cm(12") 2 pieces
④ 50cm(20")
⑤ 4cm(1 5/8")

apply glue to end of wire and insert in bead

drumstick
large beads

1cm   twist

⑤ center

3-cut beads

④

cut

⑧ SMALL DRUM

#34 wire
① 40cm(16")
② 25cm(10")
③ 30cm(12") 2 pieces
④ 20cm(8")

④

twist back and finish

make same base as for emperor

glue on

LARGE HAND DRUM

FLUTE

DRUM

RECORDER   SMALL HAND DRUM

CONTINUED ON PAGE 57

CHRISTMAS

Simple little bead crafts, such as frames and cards, that make great gifts!

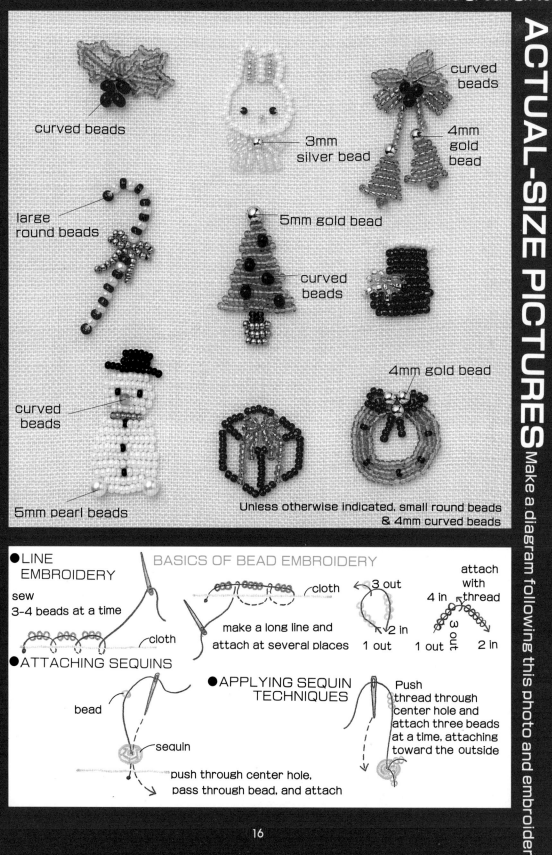

curved beads

curved beads

3mm silver bead

curved beads

4mm gold bead

large round beads

5mm gold bead

curved beads

4mm gold bead

curved beads

5mm pearl beads

Unless otherwise indicated, small round beads & 4mm curved beads

BASICS OF BEAD EMBROIDERY

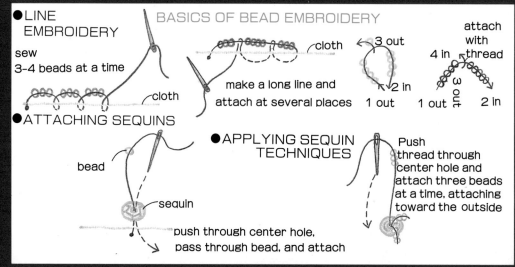

● LINE EMBROIDERY

sew 3-4 beads at a time

cloth

cloth

make a long line and attach at several places

3 out

2 in

1 out

attach with thread

4 in

3 out

1 out

2 in

● ATTACHING SEQUINS

bead

sequin

push through center hole, pass through bead, and attach

● APPLYING SEQUIN TECHNIQUES

Push thread through center hole and attach three beads at a time, attaching toward the outside

① ③ ④ ⑤ ② ⑰

INSTRUCTIONS ON PAGE 49

A tea party with ladies in long dresses.
Dolls with clay bases can be moved anywhere you like.

18

① BLUE-GREEN DRESS

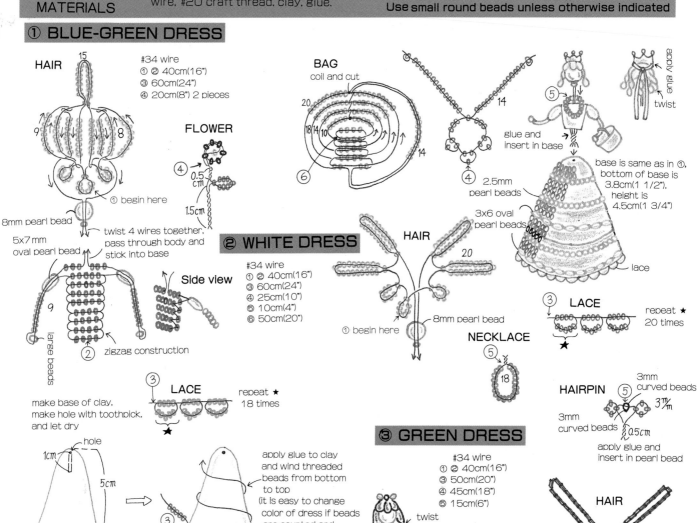

HAIR

15

#34 wire
① ② 40cm(16")
③ 60cm(24")
④ 20cm(8") 2 pieces

9   8

① begin here

FLOWER

④   0.5 cm

1.5cm

8mm pearl bead

5x7 mm oval pearl bead

twist 4 wires together, pass through body and stick into base

Side view

9

large beads

② zigzag construction

make base of clay, make hole with toothpick, and let dry

BAG
coil and cut

20

18 14 10

⑥

14

14

④

2.5mm pearl beads

3x6 oval pearl beads

⑤

glue and insert in base

apply glue

twist

base is same as in ①, bottom of base is 3.8cm(1 1/2"), height is 4.5cm(1 3/4")

lace

③ LACE   repeat ★ 20 times
★

② WHITE DRESS

#34 wire
① ② 40cm(16")
③ 60cm(24")
④ 25cm(10")
⑤ 10cm(4")
⑥ 50cm(20")

HAIR

20

① begin here

8mm pearl bead

NECKLACE

⑤

18

③ LACE   repeat ★ 18 times
★

③ GREEN DRESS

HAIRPIN   3mm curved beads

⑤   3㎜

3mm curved beads   0.5cm

apply glue and insert in pearl bead

#34 wire
① ② 40cm(16")
③ 50cm(20")
④ 45cm(18")
⑤ 15cm(6")

twist

body is same as in ⑤, bag is same as in ⑦, hem lace and body sizes are same as in ④

HAIR

20

1.5mm bugle beads

8mm pearl bead

① begin here

small beads

hole

1cm   5cm

3.6cm

twist ends of lace together and glue to base

apply glue to clay and wind threaded beads from bottom to top
(it is easy to change color of dress if beads are counted and threaded first, then glued to base)

③

twist and insert in hand

1cm

pass wires ① & ② through torso and twist, apply glue, and insert into base

twist

④ RED DRESS

#34 wire
① ② 40cm(16")
③ 50cm(20")
④ 15cm(6")

③ LACE   repeat ★ 28-33 times
★
number of beads needed depends on their shape

HAIRPIN   ④   back
front

HAIR

20

8mm pearl bead

① begin here

④ glue on

twist

torso is same as in ⑤, bottom of base: 3cm(1 1/8"), height: 3cm (1 1/8")

small beads

lace

20

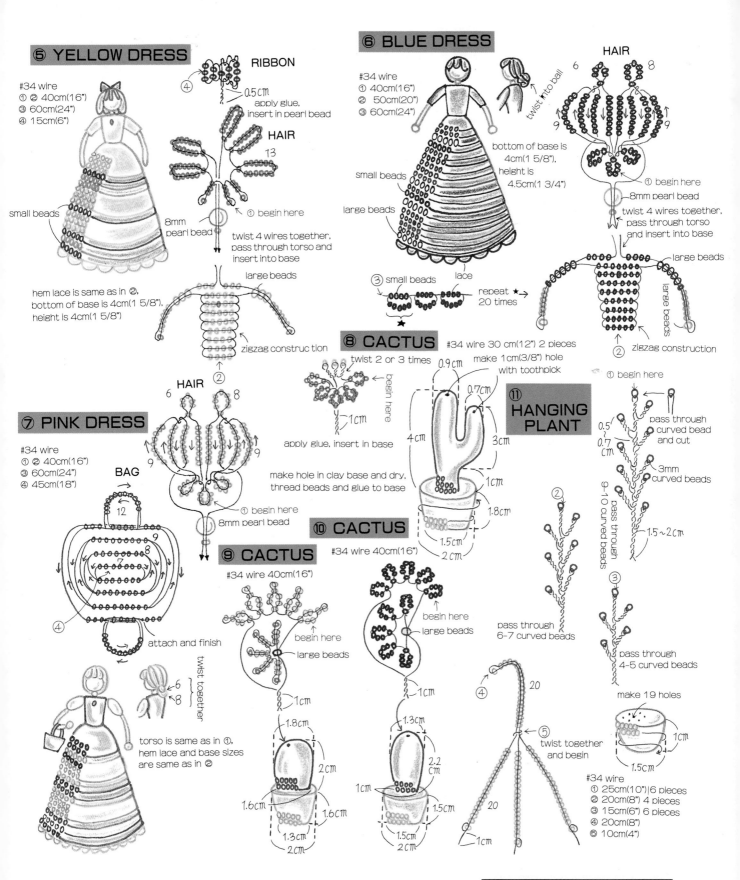

⑤ YELLOW DRESS

#34 wire
① ② 40cm(16")
③ 60cm(24")
④ 15cm(6")

RIBBON

④ 0.5cm
apply glue,
insert in pearl bead

HAIR
13

small beads

8mm
pearl bead

① begin here

twist 4 wires together,
pass through torso and
insert into base

hem lace is same as in ②,
bottom of base is 4cm(1 5/8"),
height is 4cm(1 5/8")

large beads

zigzag construction

②

⑥ BLUE DRESS

#34 wire
① 40cm(16")
② 50cm(20")
③ 60cm(24")

twist into ball

HAIR
6   8
9   9

① begin here

8mm pearl bead

twist 4 wires together,
pass through torso
and insert into base

small beads

large beads

bottom of base is
4cm(1 5/8"),
height is
4.5cm(1 3/4")

③ small beads   lace

repeat ★
20 times

★

large beads

large beads

② zigzag construction

⑦ PINK DRESS

#34 wire
① ② 40cm(16")
③ 60cm(24")
④ 45cm(18")

BAG
12

HAIR
6   8
9   9

① begin here

8mm pearl bead

④

attach and finish

twist together
6
8

torso is same as in ①,
hem lace and base sizes
are same as in ②

⑧ CACTUS

#34 wire 30 cm(12") 2 pieces

twist 2 or 3 times

begin here

1cm

apply glue, insert in base

make hole in clay base and dry,
thread beads and glue to base

0.9cm

make 1cm(3/8") hole
with toothpick

0.7cm

4cm

3cm

1cm

1.8cm

1.5cm
2 cm

⑨ CACTUS

#34 wire 40cm(16")

begin here

large beads

1cm

1.8cm

2cm

1.6cm

1.6cm

1.3cm
2cm

⑩ CACTUS

#34 wire 40cm(16")

begin here
large beads

1cm

1.3cm

2.2cm

1cm

1.5cm

1.5cm
2cm

⑪ HANGING PLANT

① begin here

pass through
curved bead
and cut

0.5
cm

0.7
cm

3mm
curved beads

1.5～2cm

②

pass through
9-10 curved beads

③

pass through
6-7 curved beads

pass through
4-5 curved beads

④   20

⑤ twist together
and begin

20

1cm

make 19 holes

1cm

1.5cm

#34 wire
① 25cm(10") 6 pieces
② 20cm(8") 4 pieces
③ 15cm(6") 6 pieces
④ 20cm(8")
⑤ 10cm(4")

CONTINUED ON PAGE 57,
⑰ CONTINUED ON PAGE 9

ANIMAL UNITED NATIONS

Chaired by the Owl, the penguin represents Antarctica
and the giraffe represents Africa

INSTRUCTIONS AND MATERIALS

small & large round beads, 3 & 4mm curved beads, 3-cut beads, 3mm bugle beads, small beads, #31 & 34 wire.

Use small round beads unless otherwise indicated

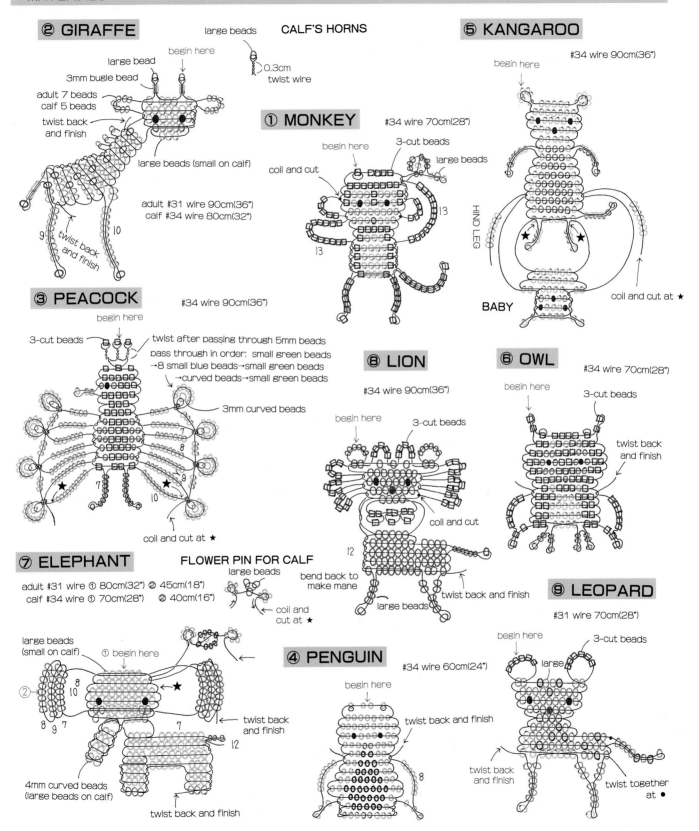

② **GIRAFFE**

large beads

CALF'S HORNS

begin here

large bead

3mm bugle bead

adult 7 beads
calf 5 beads

twist back
and finish

large beads (small on calf)

adult #31 wire 90cm(36")
calf #34 wire 80cm(32")

9   twist back   10
     and finish

0.3cm
twist wire

① **MONKEY**   #34 wire 70cm(28")

begin here

3-cut beads

large beads

coil and cut

13

13

⑤ **KANGAROO**

#34 wire 90cm(36")

begin here

HIND LEG

BABY

coil and cut at ★

③ **PEACOCK**   #34 wire 90cm(36")

3-cut beads

twist after passing through 5mm beads

pass through in order: small green beads
→8 small blue beads→small green beads
→curved beads→small green beads

3mm curved beads

7

8

7   9

10

coil and cut at ★

⑧ **LION**

#34 wire 90cm(36")

begin here

3-cut beads

coil and cut

12

bend back to
make mane

large beads

twist back and finish

⑥ **OWL**   #34 wire 70cm(28")

begin here

3-cut beads

twist back
and finish

⑨ **LEOPARD**

#31 wire 70cm(28")

⑦ **ELEPHANT**

adult #31 wire ① 80cm(32") ② 45cm(18")
calf #34 wire ① 70cm(28")   ② 40cm(16")

FLOWER PIN FOR CALF

large beads

coil and
cut at ★

large beads
(small on calf)

① begin here

★

②   8
     10

8 9 7   7

12

twist back
and finish

4mm curved beads
(large beads on calf)

twist back and finish

④ **PENGUIN**   #34 wire 60cm(24")

begin here

twist back and finish

8

begin here

large

twist back and finish

twist back
and finish

twist together
at ●

23

RABBIT FAMILY

The rabbit family always has a good time. Today they're having the bear girls over.

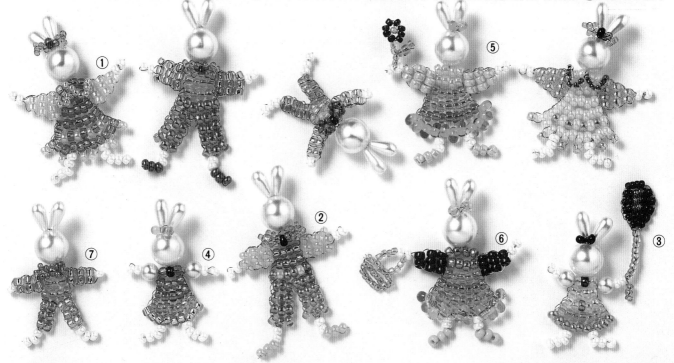

INSTRUCTIONS FOR BEAR ON PAGE 27
INSTRUCTIONS FOR POTTED PLANT ON PAGE 58

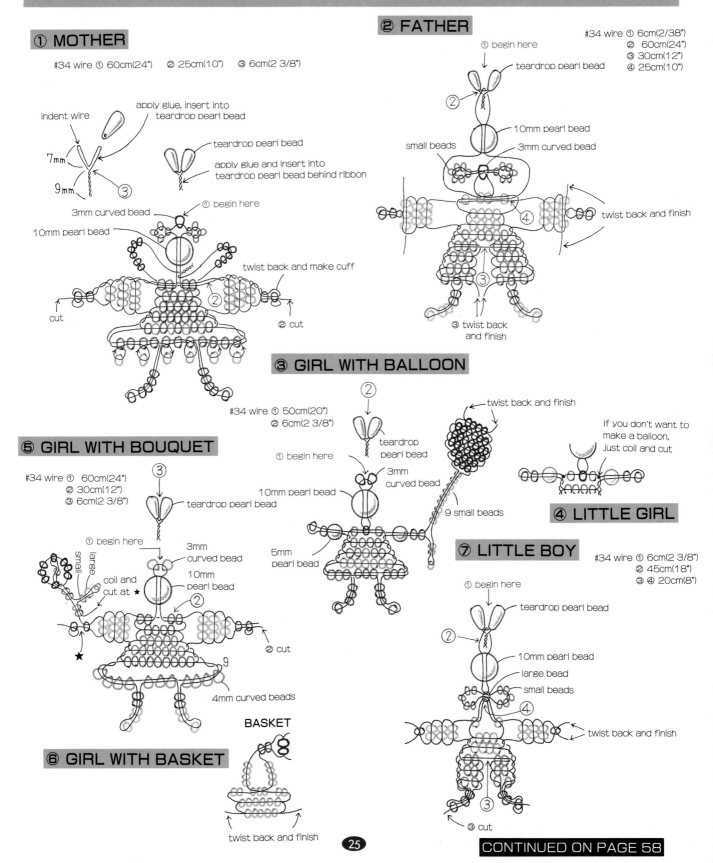

① MOTHER

#34 wire ① 60cm(24")   ② 25cm(10")   ③ 6cm(2 3/8")

indent wire

apply glue, insert into teardrop pearl bead

7mm

9mm ③

teardrop pearl bead

apply glue and insert into teardrop pearl bead behind ribbon

3mm curved bead

① begin here

10mm pearl bead

twist back and make cuff

cut ②

② cut

② FATHER

#34 wire ① 6cm(2/38")
② 60cm(24")
③ 30cm(12")
④ 25cm(10")

① begin here

② teardrop pearl bead

10mm pearl bead

small beads   3mm curved bead

④ twist back and finish

③

③ twist back and finish

③ GIRL WITH BALLOON

#34 wire ① 50cm(20")
② 6cm(2 3/8")

② teardrop pearl bead

① begin here

3mm curved bead

10mm pearl bead

5mm pearl bead

twist back and finish

9 small beads

If you don't want to make a balloon, just coil and cut

④ LITTLE GIRL

⑤ GIRL WITH BOUQUET

#34 wire ① 60cm(24")
② 30cm(12")
③ 6cm(2 3/8")

③ teardrop pearl bead

① begin here

3mm curved bead

10mm pearl bead

②

coil and cut at ★

small large

★

② cut

9

4mm curved beads

⑦ LITTLE BOY

#34 wire ① 6cm(2 3/8")
② 45cm(18")
③ ④ 20cm(8")

① begin here

② teardrop pearl bead

10mm pearl bead

large bead

small beads

④

twist back and finish

③

③ cut

BASKET

⑥ GIRL WITH BASKET

twist back and finish

25

CONTINUED ON PAGE 58

BEAR FAMILY

The fashionable bears love having guests.

Today they've invited the rabbit family from Fairyland.

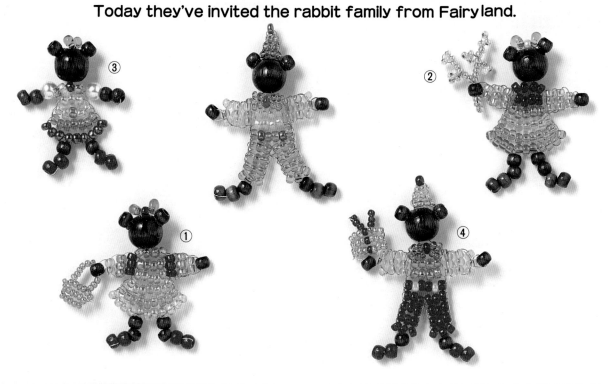

INSTRUCTIONS FOR RABBITS ON PAGE 3

INSTRUCTIONS FOR PLANTS ON PAGE 57

② FLOWER GIRL

twist

small beads

① GIRL WITH BASKET

wire ① 60cm(24") ② 30cm(12")

4mm curved beads

wood beads { R4 R10 }

① begin here

apply glue

②

twist back

7 9

R4 wood beads

twist back and finish

④ BOY WITH PRESENT

wire ① 70cm(28") ② ③ 30cm(2")

small beads

① begin here

R10 wood beads

4mm curved beads small beads

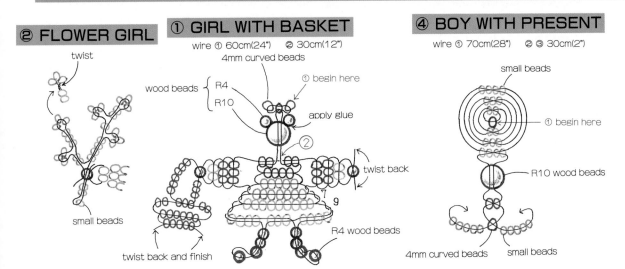

③ LITTLE GIRL

wire 45cm(18")

begin here

3mm curved beads

R4

R10 } wood beads

5mm pearl bead

twist back and finish

R4 wood beads

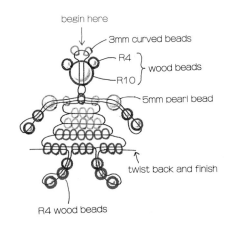

twist back and finish

R4 wood bead apply glue

③

twist back and finish

②

R4 wood beads

② twist back and finish

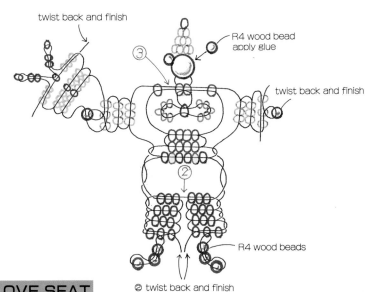

⑤ TABLE

#28 wire 100cm(40")

all wood beads

C47 R4

bend and hook

C45

coil and cut

begin here

⑥ LOVE SEAT

#28 wire 100cm(40")

all wood beads

R4 C47

coil and cut

coil and cut at ★

10

begin here

C47

★

⑦ CHAIR

#28 wire 90cm(36")

all wood beads

R4

C47

coil and cut

C47

begin here

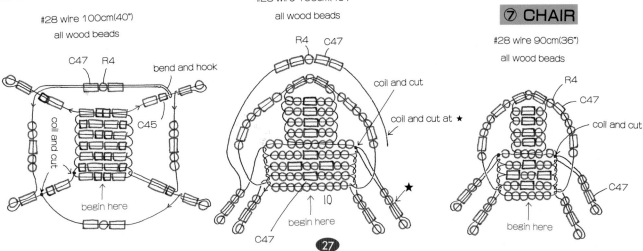

OCEAN PARADISE

The home of the mermaid is vibrant with color.
Strange fish, dolphins, and whales enjoy themselves in the coral.

12

13

14

15

16

17

18

19

20

21

22

23

INSTRUCTIONS ON PAGE 50

NAME PLATE

Arrange these beautiful letters any way you like.
Attach them to clothes, bags, or magnets.

INSTRUCTIONS ON PAGE 53

MUSICAL PARADE

Sew on to your purse or use as a brooch.

INSTRUCTIONS ON PAGE 53

DRESS UP YOUR KITCHEN

Attach these beautiful crafts to magnets to make useful decorations.

INSTRUCTIONS
AND
MATERIALS

small & large round beads, 3-cut beads, small hexagonal beads, 3 & 4mm curved beads,
small beads, 4, 8, 10, 12 & 15mm pearl beads, 3x6mm oval pearl beads, 3, 4, 6 & 7mm,
& 3x6mm colored pearl beads, 6mm rainbow pearl beads, #20 & 34 wire, #20 bead thread,
3cm(1 1/4") round, heart- & star-shaped magnets, glue.
Use small round beads unless otherwise indicated

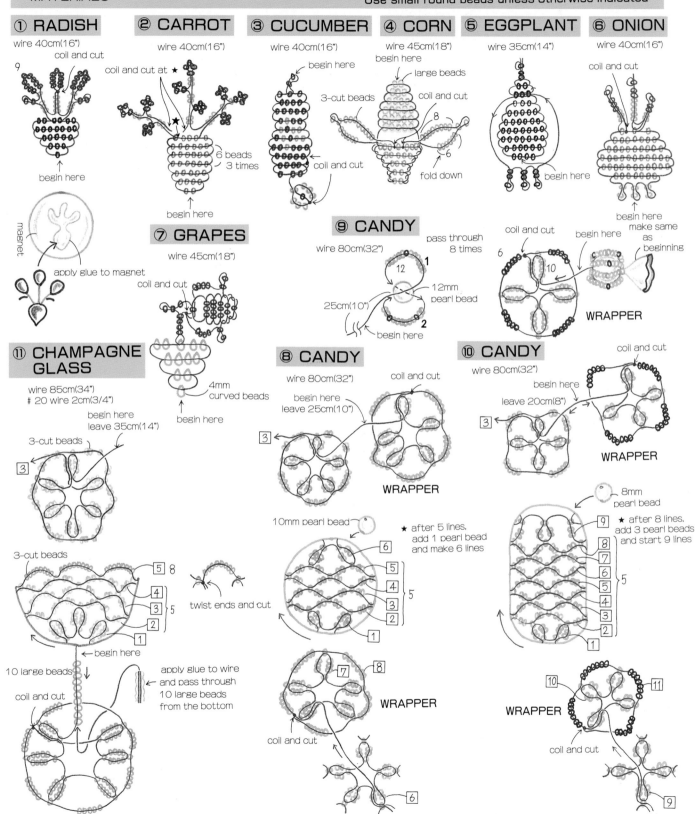

① RADISH
wire 40cm(16")
coil and cut
9
begin here
magnet
apply glue to magnet

② CARROT
wire 40cm(16")
coil and cut at ★
6 beads
3 times
begin here

③ CUCUMBER
wire 40cm(16")
begin here
coil and cut

④ CORN
wire 45cm(18")
begin here
large beads
3-cut beads
coil and cut
8
6
fold down

⑤ EGGPLANT
wire 35cm(14")
begin here

⑥ ONION
wire 40cm(16")
coil and cut
begin here
begin here
make same
as
beginning

⑦ GRAPES
wire 45cm(18")
coil and cut
4mm
curved beads
begin here

⑨ CANDY
wire 80cm(32")
pass through
8 times
12   1
12mm
pearl bead
25cm(10")
2
begin here
coil and cut
begin here
6   10
WRAPPER

⑪ CHAMPAGNE
GLASS
wire 85cm(34")
20 wire 2cm(3/4")
begin here
leave 35cm(14")
3-cut beads
3
3-cut beads
5 8
4
3   } 5
2
1
begin here
10 large beads
coil and cut
apply glue to wire
and pass through
10 large beads
from the bottom

⑧ CANDY
wire 80cm(32")
coil and cut
begin here
leave 25cm(10")
3
WRAPPER
10mm pearl bead
6
5
4   } 5
3
2
1
★ after 5 lines,
add 1 pearl bead
and make 6 lines
twist ends and cut
7   8
WRAPPER
coil and cut
6

⑩ CANDY
wire 80cm(32")
begin here
leave 20cm(8")
3
coil and cut
WRAPPER
8mm
pearl bead
9   ★ after 8 lines,
8   add 3 pearl beads
7   and start 9 lines
6
5   } 5
4
3
2
1
10   11
WRAPPER
coil and cut
9

33

SUMMER AT THE BEACH

The 3-D hat, parasol, basket, bag, and sandals are pretty accessories for your brooch or key chain.

small & large round beads. 3-cut beads. 3 & 4mm curved beads. #31 &34 wire.
Use small round beads unless otherwise indicated

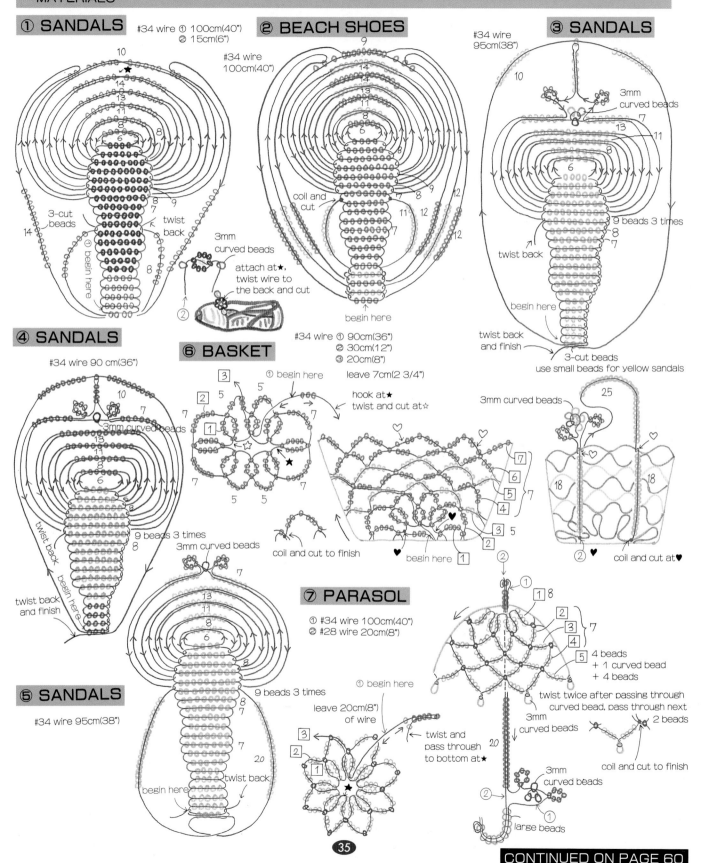

① SANDALS

#34 wire ① 100cm(40")
② 15cm(6")

10
14
13
11
8
6
8
7
3-cut beads
14
begin here
8
twist back

3mm curved beads
attach at ★, twist wire to the back and cut
②

② BEACH SHOES

#34 wire 100cm(40")

9
14
13
8
6
9
7
8
9
11 12
12
12
coil and cut
7
begin here

③ SANDALS

#34 wire 95cm(38")

10
3mm curved beads
13
7
11
8
6
9 beads 3 times
8
7
twist back
begin here
twist back and finish
3-cut beads
use small beads for yellow sandals

④ SANDALS

#34 wire 90 cm(36")

10
7
3mm curved beads
13
11
6
8
8
9 beads 3 times
8
twist back
begin here
twist back and finish

⑤ SANDALS

#34 wire 95cm(38")

13
11
8
6
3mm curved beads
7
8
7
7
9 beads 3 times
8
7
20
twist back
begin here

⑥ BASKET

#34 wire ① 90cm(36")
② 30cm(12")
③ 20cm(8")

leave 7cm(2 3/4")
hook at ★
twist and cut at ☆

① begin here
3
2
1
5
5
7
7
5
5
7

coil and cut to finish
begin here
1
2
3
5
4
5
6
7

25
3mm curved beads
18
18
② ♥
coil and cut at ♥

⑦ PARASOL

① #34 wire 100cm(40")
② #28 wire 20cm(8")

① begin here
leave 20cm(8") of wire
twist and pass through to bottom at ★
3
2
1

①
1 8
②
2
3
4
7
5
4 beads + 1 curved bead + 4 beads
twist twice after passing through curved bead, pass through next 2 beads
3mm curved beads
20
coil and cut to finish
3mm curved beads
②
① large beads

35

CONTINUED ON PAGE 60

COIN PURSE AND RINGS

Crochet after passing lace thread through beads

INSTRUCTIONS FOR SHOES ON PAGE 35
INSTRUCTIONS FOR HAT ON PAGE 60

Use large round beads unless otherwise indicated

① COIN PURSE

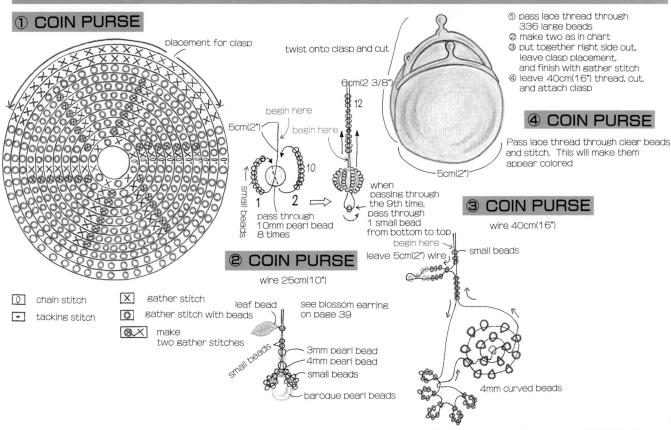

placement for clasp

twist onto clasp and cut

6cm(2 3/8")

5cm(2")

begin here

begin here

small beads

5cm(2")

1 2

pass through 10mm pearl bead 8 times

10

12

when passing through the 9th time, pass through 1 small bead from bottom to top

① pass lace thread through 336 large beads
② make two as in chart
③ put together right side out, leave clasp placement, and finish with gather stitch
④ leave 40cm(16") thread, cut, and attach clasp

④ COIN PURSE

Pass lace thread through clear beads and stitch. This will make them appear colored

③ COIN PURSE

wire 40cm(16")

begin here

leave 5cm(2") wire

small beads

② COIN PURSE

wire 25cm(10")

leaf bead

see blossom earring on page 39

small beads

3mm pearl bead
4mm pearl bead
small beads
baroque pearl beads

4mm curved beads

| 0 | chain stitch |
| - | tacking stitch |

X	gather stitch
☉	gather stitch with beads
☉X	make two gather stitches

MAKE GATHER STITCH WITH BEADS

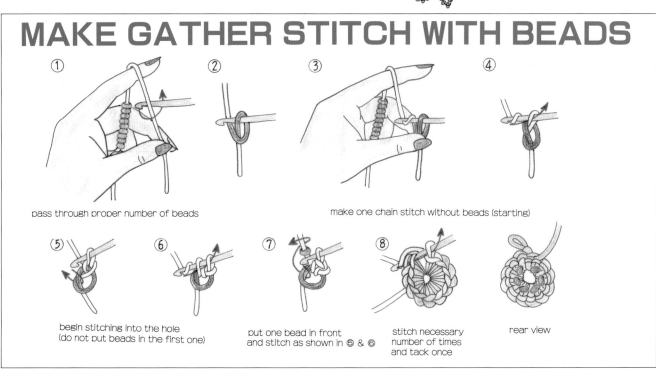

① ② ③ ④

pass through proper number of beads

make one chain stitch without beads (starting)

⑤ ⑥ ⑦ ⑧

begin stitching into the hole
(do not put beads in the first one)

put one bead in front and stitch as shown in ⑤ & ⑥

stitch necessary number of times and tack once

rear view

CONTINUED ON PAGE 11

PEARL ACCESSORIES

The bouquet ribbon works well as a barrette or brooch, the necklace goes well with a flowered blouse

INSTRUCTIONS AND MATERIALS

small & large round beads, 4mm & 5mm special large beads, 4mm curved beads, 3-cut beads, 3, 4, 5, & 8mm pearl beads, 8mm shell beads, 6x10mm & 7x12mm teardrop pearl beads, 8mm baroque pearl beads, 5mm colored pearl beads, small heart-shaped pearl beads, leaf beads, jump rings, spring rings, brooch pins, links, bails, bead tips, earring backings, large barrette, #28, #30 & 34 wire, #20 bead thread, craft filament, 4mm wide ribbon 38cm(15") long, glue. **Use small round beads unless otherwise indicated**

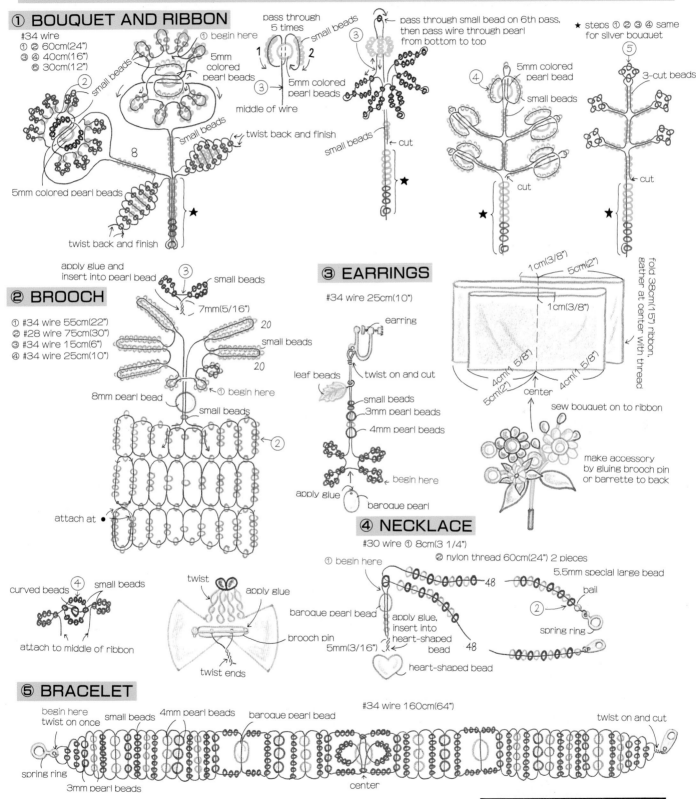

① BOUQUET AND RIBBON

#34 wire
① ② 60cm(24")
③ ④ 40cm(16")
⑤ 30cm(12")

small beads
5mm colored pearl beads
small beads
small beads
5mm colored pearl beads
twist back and finish
8
twist back and finish

pass through 5 times
small beads
5mm colored pearl beads
5mm colored pearl beads
middle of wire

pass through small bead on 6th pass, then pass wire through pearl from bottom to top
small beads
cut

★ steps ① ② ③ ④ same for silver bouquet

5mm colored pearl bead
small beads
cut

5mm colored pearl bead
small beads
3-cut beads
cut

② BROOCH

① #34 wire 55cm(22")
② #28 wire 75cm(30")
③ #34 wire 15cm(6")
④ #34 wire 25cm(10")

apply glue and insert into pearl bead
small beads
7mm(5/16")
20
small beads
20
8mm pearl bead
① begin here
small beads
attach at ●

curved beads
small beads
attach to middle of ribbon
twist
apply glue
brooch pin
5mm(3/16")
twist ends

③ EARRINGS

#34 wire 25cm(10")

earring
leaf beads
twist on and cut
small beads
3mm pearl beads
4mm pearl beads
begin here
apply glue
baroque pearl

1cm(3/8")
5cm(2")
1cm(3/8")
4cm(1 5/8")
5cm(2")
center
4cm(1 5/8")
fold 38cm(15") ribbon, gather at center with thread
sew bouquet on to ribbon
make accessory by gluing brooch pin or barrette to back

④ NECKLACE

#30 wire ① 8cm(3 1/4")
② nylon thread 60cm(24") 2 pieces

① begin here
48
5.5mm special large bead
bail
baroque pearl bead
apply glue, insert into heart-shaped bead
48
spring ring
heart-shaped bead

⑤ BRACELET

#34 wire 160cm(64")

begin here twist on once
small beads
4mm pearl beads
baroque pearl bead
twist on and cut
spring ring
3mm pearl beads
center

CONTINUED ON PAGE 61

The bracelet is easy to make and is a great present.

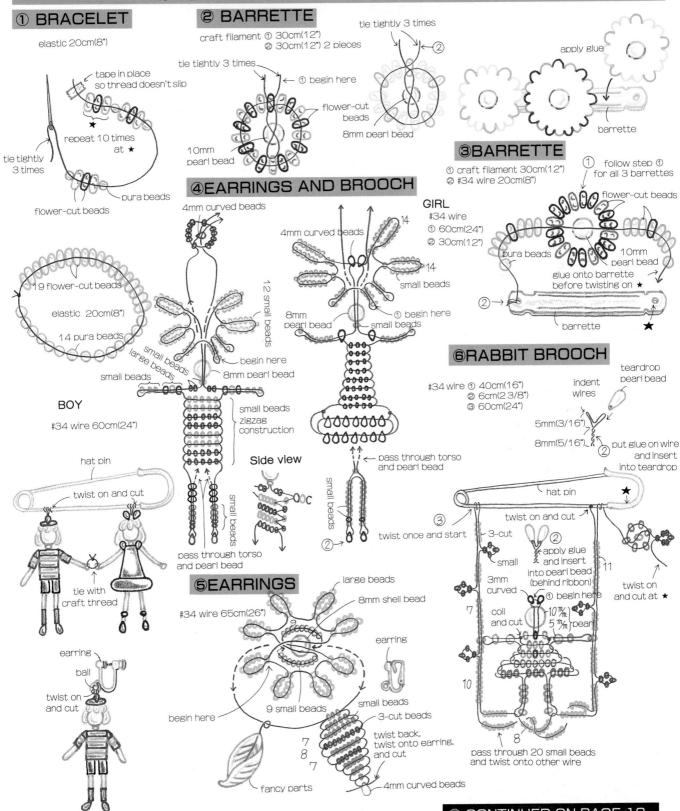

INSTRUCTIONS AND MATERIALS

small & large round beads, small beads, 3 & 4mm curved beads, small beads, 3, 4, 5, 6, 8, 10, & 12mm pearl beads, 8mm shell beads, 4x8mm teardrop pearl beads, crystal-cut beads, 5mm colored pearl beads, 6mm pura beads, rhinestone, hemisphere glass stones, leaf beads, flower-cut bead, brooch pin, hat pin, rings, earring backings, large barrette, key ring, #28, #30 & 34 wire, craft filament, elastic, glue.

① BRACELET

elastic 20cm(8")

tape in place so thread doesn't slip

tie tightly 3 times

repeat 10 times at ★

tie tightly 3 times

pura beads

flower-cut beads

② BARRETTE

craft filament ① 30cm(12")
② 30cm(12") 2 pieces

tie tightly 3 times

tie tightly 3 times

① begin here

flower-cut beads

8mm pearl bead

10mm pearl bead

apply glue

barrette

③ BARRETTE

① craft filament 30cm(12")
② #34 wire 20cm(8")

① follow step ① for all 3 barrettes

flower-cut beads

pura beads

10mm pearl bead

glue onto barrette before twisting on ★

barrette ★

④ EARRINGS AND BROOCH

4mm curved beads

4mm curved beads

14

14

small beads

① begin here

8mm pearl bead

small beads

12 small beads

begin here

8mm pearl bead

small beads large beads

small beads

BOY

#34 wire 60cm(24")

hat pin

twist on and cut

tie with craft thread

small beads zigzag construction

Side view

small beads

pass through torso and pearl bead

pass through torso and pearl bead

small beads

twist once and start

②

⑤ EARRINGS

large beads

8mm shell bead

#34 wire 65cm(26")

earring

earring

bail

twist on and cut

begin here

9 small beads

small beads

3-cut beads

twist back, twist onto earring, and cut

7 8 7

4mm curved beads

fancy parts

GIRL

#34 wire
① 60cm(24")
② 30cm(12")

⑥ RABBIT BROOCH

#34 wire ① 40cm(16")
② 6cm(2 3/8")
③ 60cm(24")

teardrop pearl bead

indent wires

5mm(3/16")

8mm(5/16")

② put glue on wire and insert into teardrop

hat pin ★

twist on and cut

③

3-cut

small

3mm curved

② apply glue and insert into pearl bead (behind ribbon)

① begin here

10mm

5mm pearl

11

twist on and cut at ★

coil and cut

7

10

8

pass through 20 small beads and twist onto other wire

19 flower-cut beads

elastic 20cm(8")

14 pura beads

earring

bail

twist on and cut

⑧ CONTINUED ON PAGE 13
⑨ ⑩ CONTINUED ON PAGE 43

POUCH AND ACCESSORIES

The silver cat is made with easy embroidery.
Slightly large square beads in the necklace project a mature image.

42

INSTRUCTIONS AND MATERIALS

small & large round beads, small beads, small hexagonal beads, 3 & 4mm curved beads, small beads, 4, 8, 10, 12 & 15mm pearl beads, 4mm purakatto beads, 4.6mm rhinestone, 4.6mm hemisphere glass stone beads, 9mm mirror Jewelry, spring rings, brooch pin, hat pin, rings, large barrette, #28 & 34 wire, craft filament, plastic board, glue.

Use large round beads unless otherwise indicated

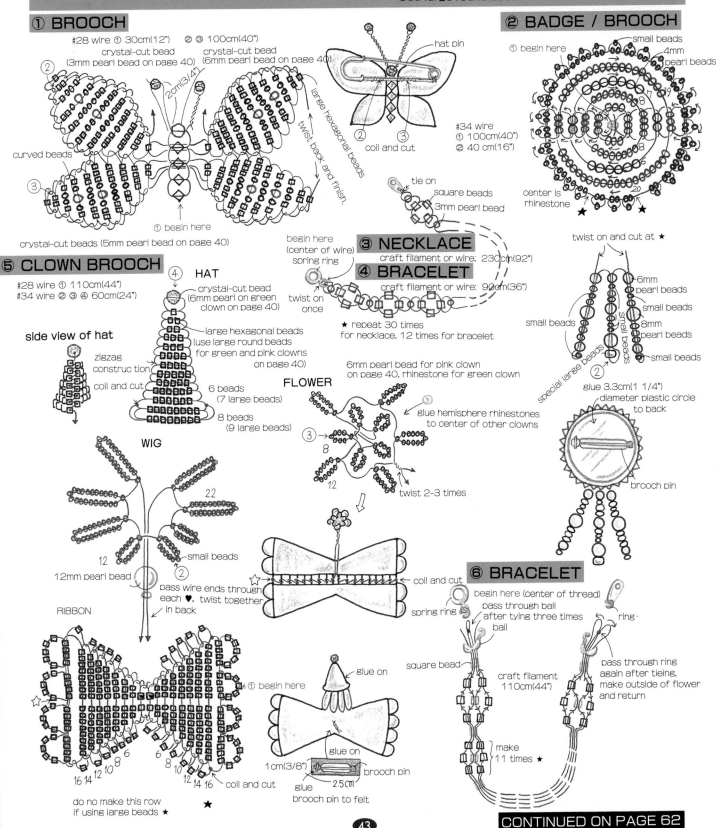

① BROOCH

#28 wire ① 30cm(12") ② ③ 100cm(40")
crystal-cut bead
(3mm pearl bead on page 40)
crystal-cut bead
(6mm pearl bead on page 40)

②
③
2cm(3/4")
① begin here

curved beads

large hexagonal beads
twist back and finish.

crystal-cut beads (5mm pearl bead on page 40)

hat pin
② ③
coil and cut

② BADGE / BROOCH

① begin here
small beads
4mm
pearl beads

#34 wire
① 100cm(40")
② 40 cm(16")

center is rhinestone

③ NECKLACE

craft filament or wire: 230cm(92")

④ BRACELET

craft filament or wire: 90cm(36")

begin here
(center of wire)
spring ring
twist on once

tie on
square beads
3mm pearl bead

★ repeat 30 times
for necklace, 12 times for bracelet

twist on and cut at ★

6mm pearl beads
small beads
8mm pearl beads
small beads
small beads
②
special large beads

glue 3.3cm(1 1/4")
diameter plastic circle to back

brooch pin

⑤ CLOWN BROOCH

#28 wire ① 110cm(44")
#34 wire ② ③ ④ 60cm(24")

side view of hat

zigzag construction
coil and cut

④ HAT
crystal-cut bead
(6mm pearl on green clown on page 40)

large hexagonal beads
(use large round beads for green and pink clowns on page 40)

6 beads
(7 large beads)

8 beads
(9 large beads)

WIG

22
12
small beads
②
12mm pearl bead

RIBBON

pass wire ends through each ♥, twist together in back

① begin here
16 14 12 10 8 6
8 10
12 14 16
coil and cut

do no make this row
if using large beads ★

6mm pearl bead for pink clown on page 40, rhinestone for green clown

FLOWER

glue hemisphere rhinestones to center of other clowns

①
③
8
12
twist 2-3 times

coil and cut

spring ring

glue on

glue on

1cm(3/8")
2.5cm
glue
brooch pin to felt

brooch pin

⑥ BRACELET

begin here (center of thread)
pass through bail after tying three times
bail
ring

square bead

craft filament 110cm(44")

pass through ring again after tieing, make outside of flower and return

make 11 times ★

43

CONTINUED ON PAGE 62
CONTINUED ON PAGE 62

BEAD BASICS

TYPES OF BEADS

BEADS

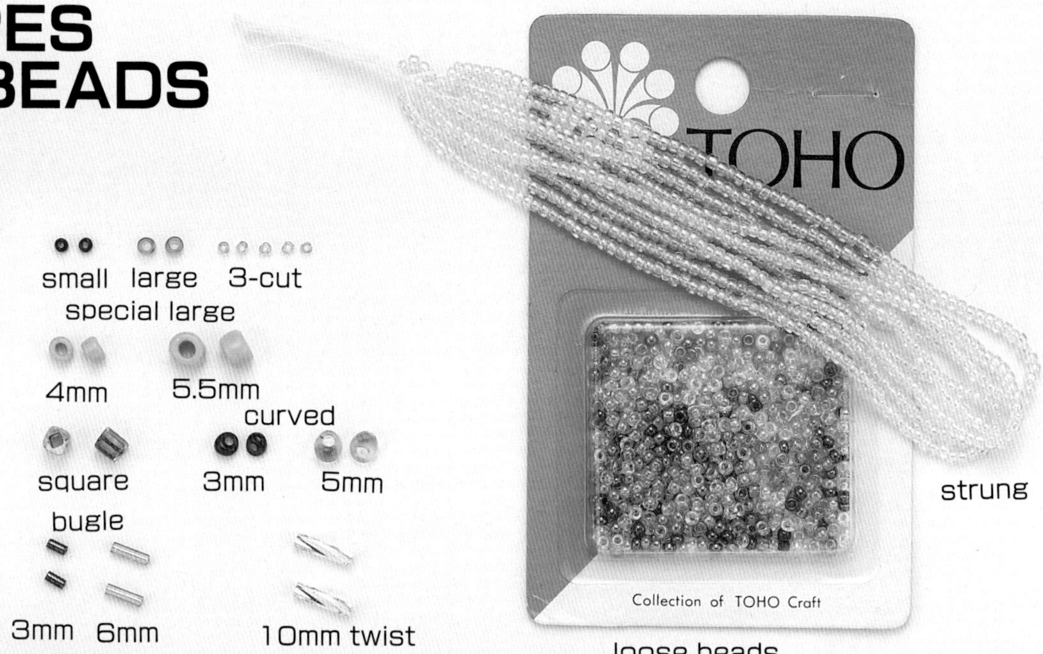

small large 3-cut
special large

4mm   5.5mm
         curved

square   3mm   5mm
bugle

3mm 6mm   10mm twist

strung

loose beads

Collection of TOHO Craft

PEARL BEADS

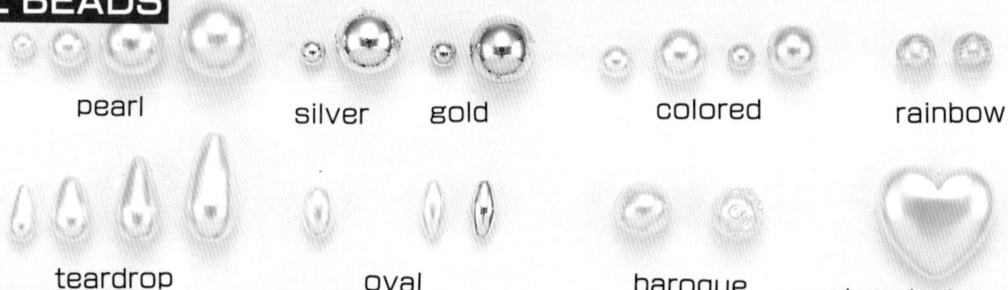

pearl   silver gold   colored   rainbow

teardrop oval   baroque heart-shaped
                           (half-drilled)

WOOD BEADS

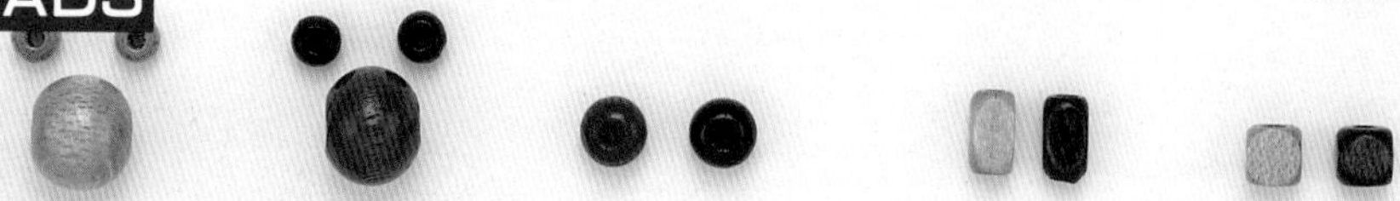

4x7mm   5x5mm

PARTS

rhinestones   crystal-cut   sequins

hemisphere acrylic   leaf   bell   flower-cut
pearl stone mirror-cut

FINDINGS FOR ACCESSORIES

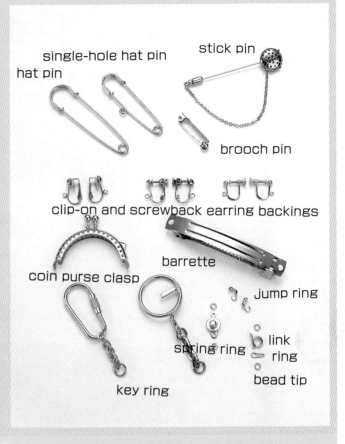

single-hole hat pin
stick pin
hat pin
brooch pin
clip-on and screwback earring backings
coin purse clasp
barrette
jump ring
spring ring
link ring
bead tip
key ring

WIRE, CRAFT FILAMENTS AND TOOLS

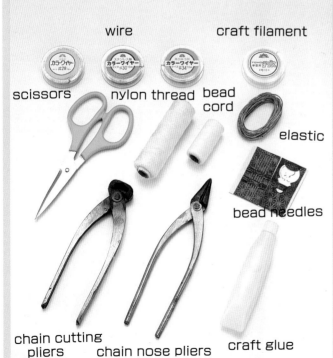

wire
craft filament
scissors
nylon thread
bead cord
elastic
bead needles
chain cutting pliers
chain nose pliers
craft glue

WIRE
Use wire to make miniatures.
10m(33ft) rolls of various thickness; #28, #30, and # 34 are sold for use in different crafts. Be careful not to bend the wire too hard or it may break.

CRAFT FILAMENT
Use for necklaces or rings.
Glue on knots so they don't come off.

SCISSORS AND PLIERS
Use Cutting pliers to cut thick wires and scissors to cut craft filament.
Chain nose pliers are useful for opening and closing jump rings

NYLON THREAD AND BEAD CORD
These are strong for beading and useful for accessories and embroidery as well.

ELASTIC
Thin elastic is used for making bracelets and sleeeve holders.

BEAD NEEDLES
Needles for fine beads, accessories and embroidery.

CRAFT GLUE
Glue used for beads and knots in crafts.
If not available, use a glue that dries clear.

LAURA AND MARY

MARY **LAURA**

Practice with these lessons and learn the basics of beadwork.

① Cut wire to proper size.
   Start at middle of wire unless otherwise indicated.
② Wires must intersect inside beads for craft to lie flat.
③ Wire is drawn loose in pictures to see instructions clearly. Tighten it as you proceed.

For crafts with several colors, see photos for proper selection.

MATERIALS
   small round beads,
   4mm curved beads,
   3-cut beads,
   8mm pearl beads,
   #34 wire,
   craft glue

Use small round beads unless otherwise indicated.

❶ wire ① 75cm(30") ② 40cm(16")

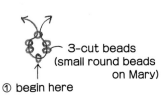

3-cut beads
(small round beads on Mary)

① begin here

begin at middle of wire ①

❷

curved beads

BACK HAIR

BANGS →

14

← begin here

tighten wire to make hair

❸

pearl bead

apply glue

Pass through face pearl and neck pearl first. Put glue on top of head pearl and adjust hair. Use only glue that dries clear.

❹

large beads

make lace

7
10
12

pass through lace and make legs

large beads

Tighten wire to make body, skirt, hem lace, and legs. Twist back to edge of body and cut.

❺

cut

large beads

wrap around bead once and cut

②

Make arms with wire ②. Begin from middle of wire, make the left side, pass two wires through body, and make right side.

Change color of beads according to the photo of Mary.

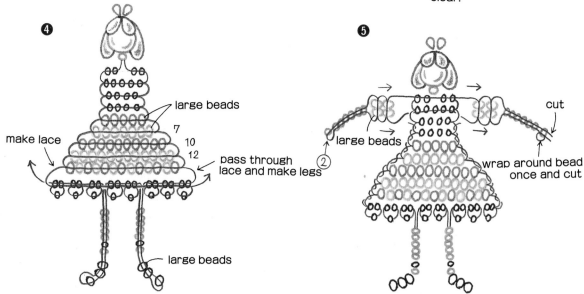

MAKE A BASKET!

① Let's practice making 3-d crafts with this basket. Make the flat bottom first, then the sides.
② Two wires pass through at points marked ★ and ☆. Follow the pattern carefully.
③ Make handle and flower. Twist the ends of the wires together and cut.

MATERIALS #34 wire
small round beads,
large round beads,
4mm curved beads.
Use small round beads unless otherwise indicated

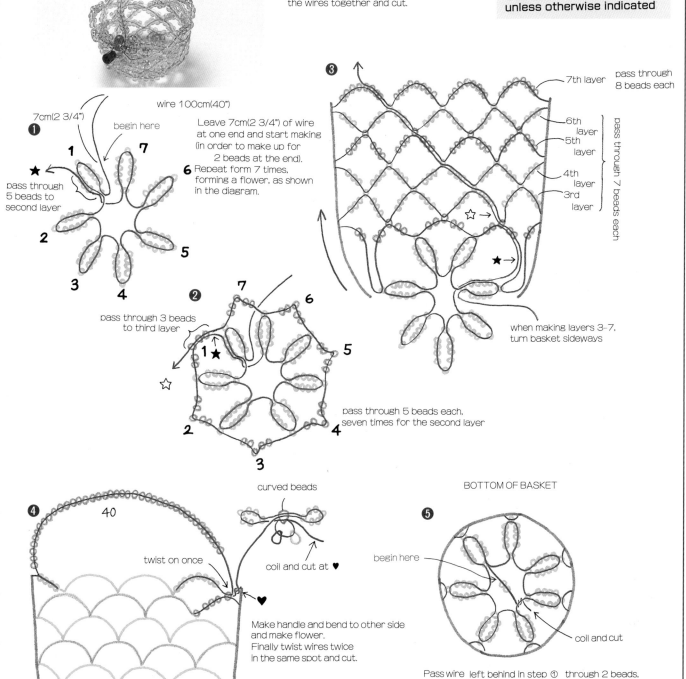

wire 100cm(40")

Leave 7cm(2 3/4") of wire at one end and start making (in order to make up for 2 beads at the end).
Repeat form 7 times, forming a flower, as shown in the diagram.

①
7cm(2 3/4")
begin here
1 7
★
pass through 5 beads to second layer
2
3
4 5

②
7
6
1 ★
5
pass through 3 beads to third layer
☆
2
4
3
pass through 5 beads each, seven times for the second layer

③
7th layer — pass through 8 beads each
6th layer
5th layer
4th layer
3rd layer
pass through 7 beads each
☆→
★→
when making layers 3-7, turn basket sideways

④
40
twist on once
curved beads
coil and cut at ♥
♥
Make handle and bend to other side and make flower.
Finally twist wires twice in the same spot and cut.

⑤ BOTTOM OF BASKET
begin here
coil and cut
Pass wire left behind in step ① through 2 beads, attach to other side, and cut.

POINTS TO REMEMBER

MOVING BEADS

● Passing wire taut loose beads

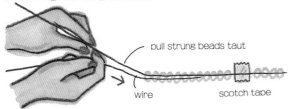

move beads with fingertips

● Wiring strung beads

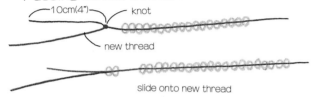

pull strung beads taut

wire

scotch tape

● Passing thread through strung beads

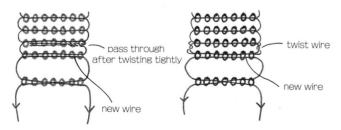

—10cm(4")— knot

new thread

slide onto new thread

CHANGING WIRES

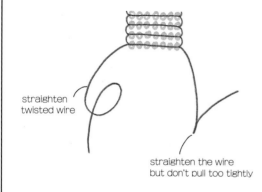

pass through after twisting tightly

twist wire

new wire

new wire

IF THE WIRE BREAKS!

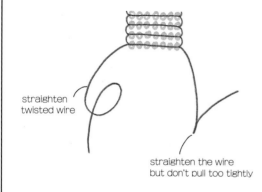

straighten twisted wire

straighten the wire
but don't pull too tightly

FINISHING (WIRE)

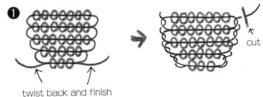

❶

cut

twist back and finish

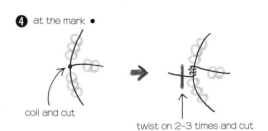

❷

twist flat in back
and cut

❸

cut

❹ at the mark ●

coil and cut

twist on 2-3 times and cut

FINISHING AT FINDINGS

● Jump rings

△　✗

● bead tip

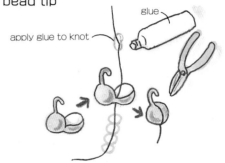

glue

apply glue to knot

INSTRUCTIONS AND MATERIALS

small & large round beads, small beads, 4mm curved beads, large triangular beads, 3, 4, 5, & 7mm pearl beads, R4 wood beads, 5 & 6mm sequins, 6.4mm rhinestones, brooch pin, single-hole hat pin, earrings, 8mm bell, #28, 30 & 34 wire, plastic board, 20x25cm[8x10"] black cotton cloth, 19x24cm[7 1/2"x 9 1/2"] frame, glue.

Use large round beads unless otherwise indicated

① CHRISTMAS TREE IN FRAME

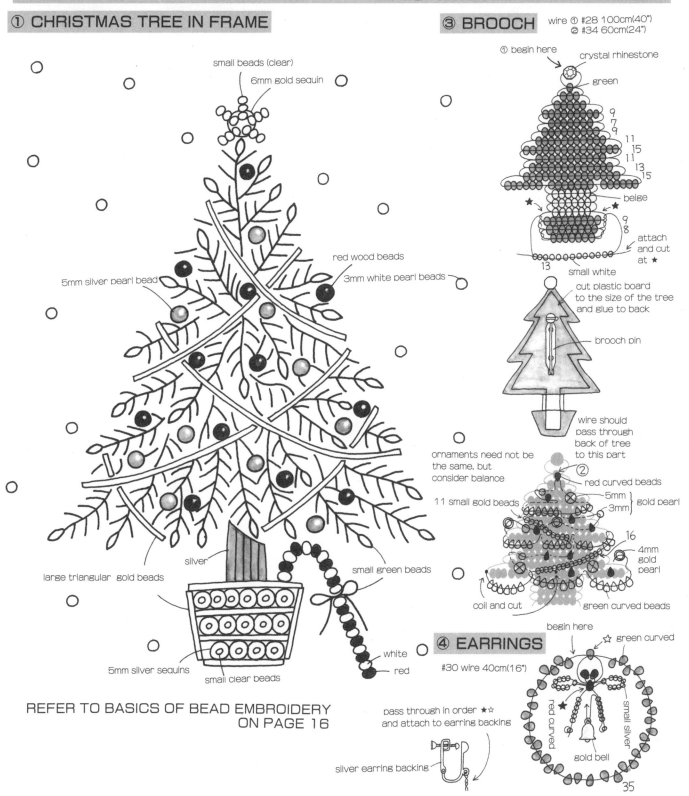

small beads (clear)
6mm gold sequin
red wood beads
3mm white pearl beads
5mm silver pearl bead
silver
red wood beads
small green beads
large triangular gold beads
5mm silver sequins
small clear beads
white
red

REFER TO BASICS OF BEAD EMBROIDERY
ON PAGE 16

③ BROOCH

wire ① #28 100cm(40")
② #34 60cm(24")

① begin here
crystal rhinestone
green
9
7
9
11
15
11
13
15
beige
9
8
attach and cut at ★
13
small white

cut plastic board to the size of the tree and glue to back
brooch pin
wire should pass through back of tree to this part

ornaments need not be the same, but consider balance

② red curved beads
5mm } gold pearl
3mm
11 small gold beads
16
4mm gold pearl
coil and cut
green curved beads

④ EARRINGS

#30 wire 40cm(16")

begin here
green curved
red curved
small silver
gold bell
35

pass through in order ★☆
and attach to earring backing

silver earring backing

② CHRISTMAS WREATH

wire ① #30 140cm(56") ② #28 30cm(12")
③ #34 70cm(28") ④ #34 30cm(12")
① begin here leave 7cm(2 3/4") of wire

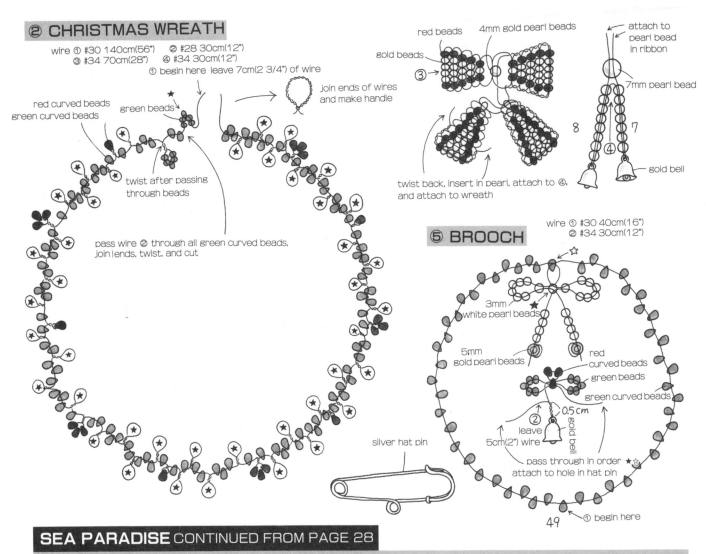

join ends of wires and make handle

red curved beads
green curved beads

green beads

twist after passing through beads

pass wire ② through all green curved beads, join ends, twist, and cut

red beads
4mm gold pearl beads
gold beads
③

attach to pearl bead in ribbon

7mm pearl bead

8 ④ 7

gold bell

twist back, insert in pearl, attach to ④, and attach to wreath

⑤ BROOCH

wire ① #30 40cm(16")
② #34 30cm(12")

3mm white pearl beads
★
5mm gold pearl beads
red curved beads
green beads
green curved beads
② 0.5cm
leave 5cm(2") wire
gold bell
pass through in order ★ ☆
attach to hole in hat pin

49 ① begin here

silver hat pin

SEA PARADISE CONTINUED FROM PAGE 28

| INSTRUCTIONS AND MATERIALS | small & large round beads, 4mm curved beads, 3m & 6mm bugle beads, 8mm pearl beads, 6mm sequins, #34 wire, clay, glue. Use large round beads unless otherwise indicated |

⑮ STRIPED SEA BASS

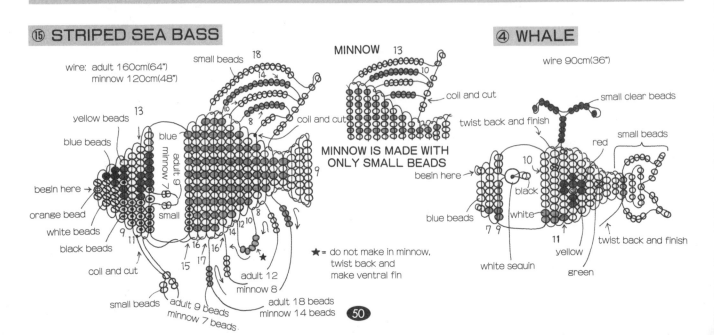

wire: adult 160cm(64")
minnow 120cm(48")

small beads 18
14
yellow beads 13
blue beads
blue
adult 9
minnow 7
begin here →
orange bead
white beads
black beads 9
coil and cut 11
15 17
16 16
14
adult 12
minnow 8
9
small beads
adult 9 beads
minnow 7 beads
adult 18 beads
minnow 14 beads

MINNOW 13
10
coil and cut

MINNOW IS MADE WITH ONLY SMALL BEADS

★ = do not make in minnow, twist back and make ventral fin

④ WHALE

wire 90cm(36")

small clear beads
twist back and finish
red
small beads
10
begin here
black
blue beads
white
7 9
white sequin
11
yellow
green
twist back and finish

50

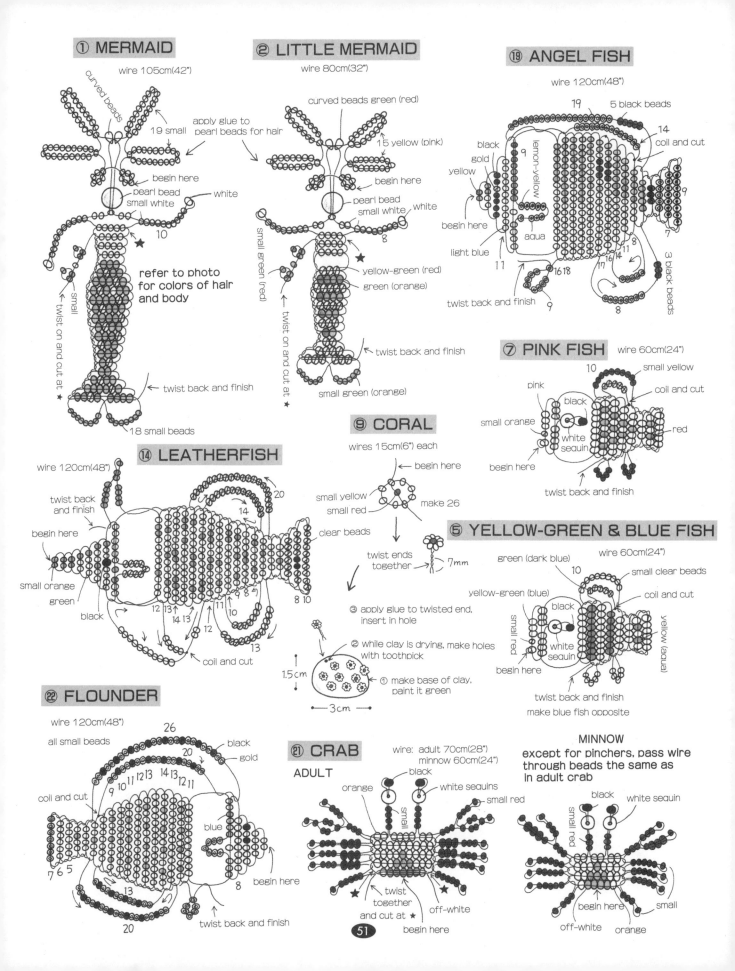

① MERMAID

wire 105cm(42")

curved beads

19 small

apply glue to pearl beads for hair

begin here

pearl bead small white

white

10

★

small

twist on and cut at ★

refer to photo for colors of hair and body

twist back and finish

18 small beads

② LITTLE MERMAID

wire 80cm(32")

curved beads green (red)

15 yellow (pink)

begin here

pearl bead small white

white

8

small green (red)

twist on and cut at ★

★

yellow-green (red)

green (orange)

twist back and finish

small green (orange)

⑲ ANGEL FISH

wire 120cm(48")

19

5 black beads

14

coil and cut

black
gold
yellow

lemon-yellow

begin here

aqua

light blue

11

11

twist back and finish

9

16 18

17

14

7

9

3 black beads

8

⑭ LEATHERFISH

wire 120cm(48")

twist back and finish

begin here

small orange

green

black

20

14

clear beads

12 13

14 13

12

11

10

13

coil and cut

8 9 8

8 10

⑨ CORAL

wires 15cm(6") each

begin here

small yellow

small red

make 26

twist ends together

7mm

③ apply glue to twisted end, insert in hole

② while clay is drying, make holes with toothpick

① make base of clay, paint it green

1.5cm

3cm

⑦ PINK FISH

wire 60cm(24")

10

small yellow

coil and cut

pink

black

small orange

white sequin

red

begin here

twist back and finish

⑤ YELLOW-GREEN & BLUE FISH

wire 60cm(24")

green (dark blue)

10

small clear beads

yellow-green (blue)

coil and cut

black

small red

white sequin

yellow (aqua)

begin here

twist back and finish

make blue fish opposite

㉒ FLOUNDER

wire 120cm(48")

all small beads

26

20

black

gold

9 10 11 12 13 14 13 12 11

coil and cut

blue

7 6 5

13

begin here

8

twist back and finish

20

㉑ CRAB

wire: adult 70cm(28")
minnow 60cm(24")

ADULT

orange

black

white sequins

small

small red

twist together and cut at ★

begin here

★

★

MINNOW

except for pinchers, pass wire through beads the same as in adult crab

black

white sequin

small red

begin here

small

off-white

orange

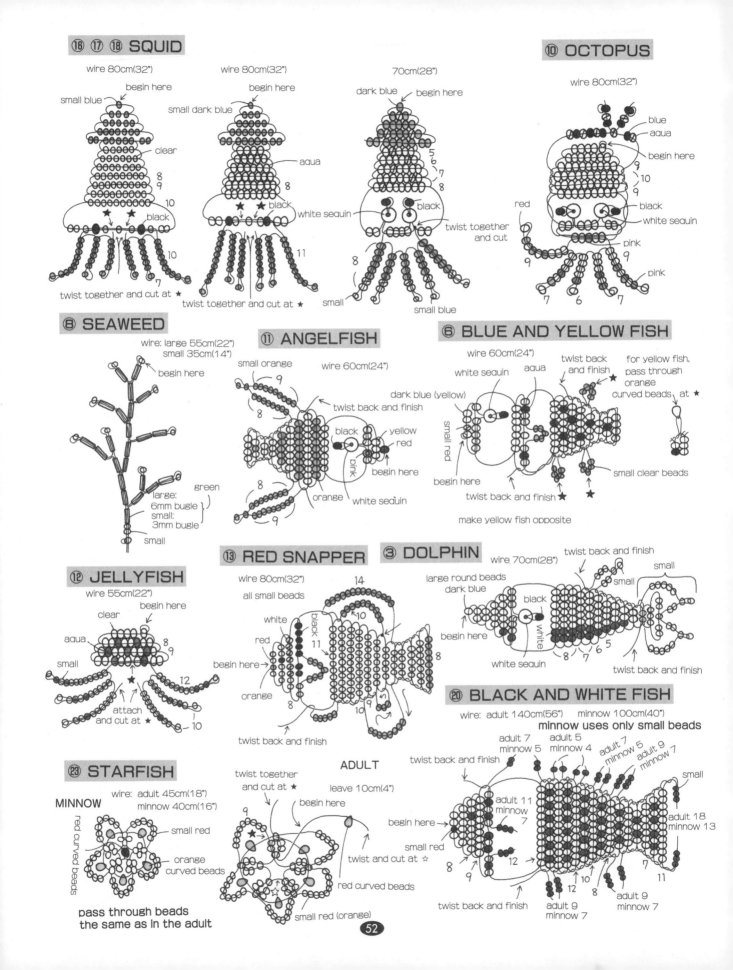

⑯ ⑰ ⑱ SQUID

wire 80cm(32")
begin here
small blue
clear
8
9
10
black
10
7
twist together and cut at ★

wire 80cm(32")
begin here
small dark blue
aqua
8
black
white sequin
11
twist together and cut at ★

70cm(28")
dark blue
begin here
5
6
7
8
black
twist together and cut
8
small
small blue

⑩ OCTOPUS

wire 80cm(32")
blue
aqua
begin here
9
10
9
red
black
white sequin
pink
9
pink
9
7
6
7

⑧ SEAWEED

wire: large 55cm(22")
small 35cm(14")
begin here
large:
6mm bugle
small:
3mm bugle
green
small

⑪ ANGELFISH

small orange
9
8
wire 60cm(24")
twist back and finish
black
yellow
red
pink
begin here
8
orange
white sequin
9

⑥ BLUE AND YELLOW FISH

wire 60cm(24")
white sequin
aqua
twist back and finish
for yellow fish,
pass through
orange
curved beads
at ★
small red
dark blue (yellow)
begin here
twist back and finish ★
small clear beads
make yellow fish opposite

⑫ JELLYFISH

wire 55cm(22")
clear
begin here
aqua
8
9
small
12
attach
and cut at ★
10

⑬ RED SNAPPER

wire 80cm(32")
all small beads
14
white
black
red
11
begin here →
orange
8
10
9
8
twist back and finish

③ DOLPHIN

wire 70cm(28")
twist back and finish
large round beads
dark blue
small
small
black
begin here
white
white sequin
8
7
6
5
twist back and finish

⑳ BLACK AND WHITE FISH

wire: adult 140cm(56")   minnow 100cm(40")
minnow uses only small beads
twist back and finish
adult 7
minnow 5
adult 5
minnow 4
adult 7
minnow 5
adult 9
minnow 7
small
adult 11
minnow
begin here
small red
8
9
12
adult 18
minnow 13
10
12
7
8
11
twist back and finish
adult 9
minnow 7
adult 9
minnow 7

㉓ STARFISH

MINNOW
wire: adult 45cm(18")
minnow 40cm(16")
red curved beads
small red
orange
curved beads
pass through beads
the same as in the adult

ADULT
twist together
and cut at ★
leave 10cm(4")
begin here
9
twist and cut at ☆
red curved beads
small red (orange)

INSTRUCTIONS AND MATERIALS	small & large round beads, 4mm special large beads, 3mm curved beads, 5 & 10mm pearl beads, 4x8mm teardrop pearl beads, #30 & 34 wire, #20 bead thread, nameplate kit. glue. **Use large round beads unless otherwise indicated**

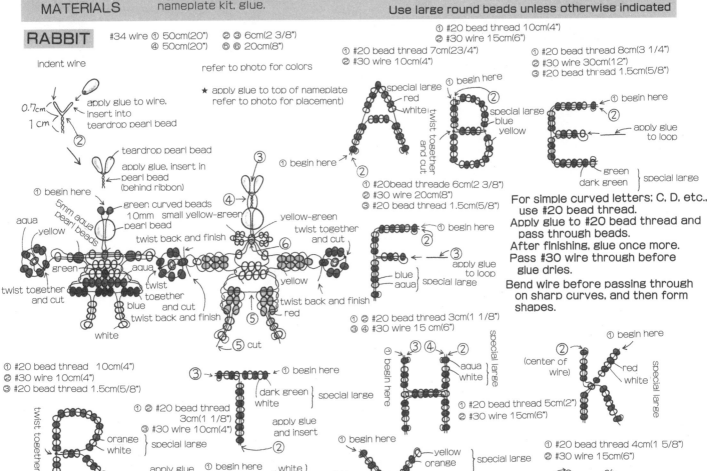

RABBIT

#34 wire ① 50cm(20") ② ③ 6cm(2 3/8")
④ 50cm(20") ⑤ ⑥ 20cm(8")

refer to photo for colors

indent wire

0.7cm 1cm apply glue to wire, insert into teardrop pearl bead ②

teardrop pearl bead
apply glue, insert in pearl bead (behind ribbon)

① begin here

5mm aqua pearl beads green curved beads 10mm small yellow-green pearl bead

aqua yellow twist back and finish

green aqua twist together and cut

twist together and cut twist blue together and cut yellow twist back and finish red ⑤ ⑤ cut

twist back and finish white

★ apply glue to top of nameplate refer to photo for placement)

① #20 bead thread 10cm(4")
② #30 wire 10cm(4")
③ #20 bead thread 1.5cm(5/8")

③ ④ ⑥ ① begin here yellow-green twist together and cut

A ① begin here special large red white ② twist together and cut

B ① begin here ② special large blue yellow

E ① begin here ② apply glue to loop green dark green } special large

① #20 bead thread 10cm(4")
② #30 wire 15cm(6")

① #20 bead thread 7cm(23/4")
② #30 wire 10cm(4")

① #20 bead thread 8cm(3 1/4")
② #30 wire 30cm(12")
③ #20 bead thread 1.5cm(5/8")

For simple curved letters; C, D, etc., use #20 bead thread.
Apply glue to #20 bead thread and pass through beads.
After finishing, glue once more.
Pass #30 wire through before glue dries.
Bend wire before passing through on sharp curves, and then form shapes.

F ① begin here ② ③ apply glue to loop blue aqua } special large

① #20 bead threade 6cm(2 3/8")
② #30 wire 20cm(8")
③ #20 bead thread 1.5cm(5/8")

T ③ ① begin here dark green white } special large apply glue and insert ②

① ② #20 bead thread 3cm(1 1/8")
③ ④ #30 wire 15 cm(6")

H ③ ④ ② begin here begin here aqua white } special large ① #20 bead thread 5cm(2") ② #30 wire 15cm(6")

K ① begin here ② (center of wire) red white } special large

R twist together orange white } special large ① begin here ②

① #20 bead thread 10cm(4")
② #30 wire 10cm(4")
③ #20 bead thread 1.5cm(5/8")

① #20 bead thread 8cm(3 1/4")
② #30 wire 15cm(6")

3 ① ② #20 bead thread 3cm(1 1/8") ③ #30 wire 10cm(4") apply glue to loop ② center of wire ① begin here white blue } special large twist together and cut

X ① begin here yellow orange } special large ① #20 bead thread 4cm(1 5/8") ② #30 wire 25cm(10") ② (center of wire)

Y ① #20 bead thread 4cm(1 5/8") ② #30 wire 15cm(6") ② (center of wire) ① begin here yellow blue } special large

---

INSTRUCTIONS AND MATERIALS	small & large round beads, 4mm special large beads, 3 & 4mm pearl beads, 8mm baroque pearl beads, #28 & #31 wire, #20 bead thread, glue **Use large round beads unless otherwise indicated.**

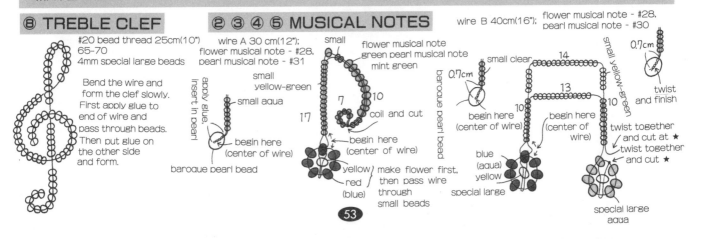

⑧ TREBLE CLEF

#20 bead thread 25cm(10")
65-70
4mm special large beads

Bend the wire and form the clef slowly. First apply glue to end of wire and pass through beads. Then put glue on the other side and form.

② ③ ④ ⑤ MUSICAL NOTES

wire A 30 cm(12");
flower musical note - #28,
pearl musical note - #31

small small yellow-green small aqua apply glue, insert in pearl begin here (center of wire) baroque pearl bead

17 7 10 flower musical note green pearl musical note mint green coil and cut begin here (center of wire) make flower first, then pass wire through small beads yellow red (blue)

wire B 40cm(16"); flower musical note - #28, pearl musical note - #30

small clear 0.7cm twist and finish small yellow-green

baroque pearl bead 0.7cm 14 13 10 10 begin here (center of wire) begin here (center of wire) twist together and cut at ★ twist together and cut ★

blue (aqua) yellow special large

special large aqua

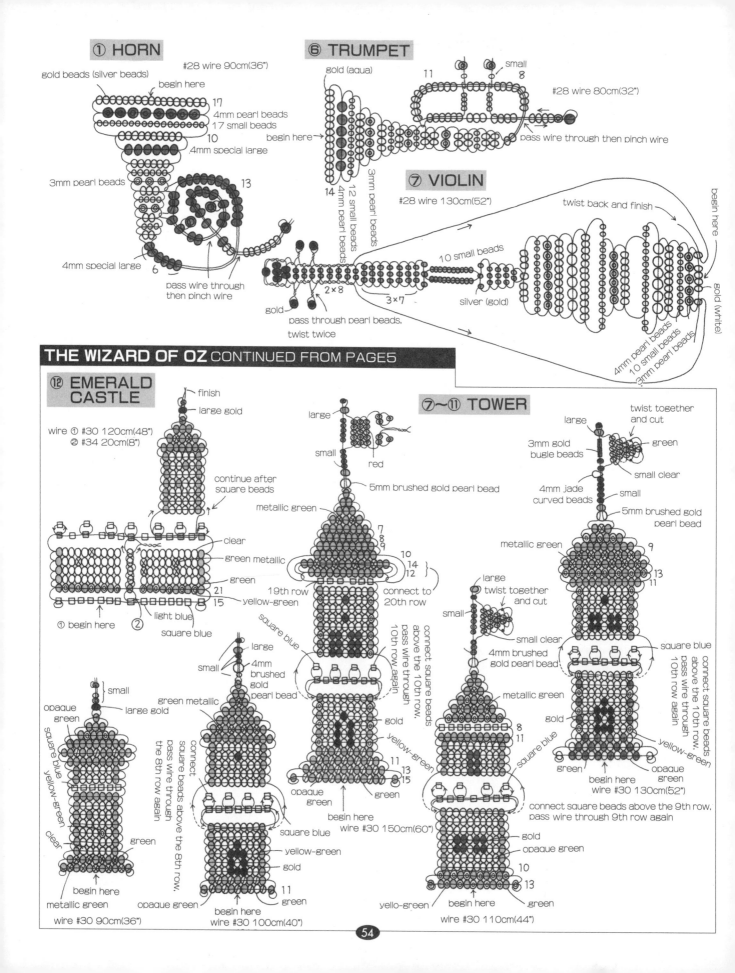

① HORN

#28 wire 90cm(36")

gold beads (silver beads)
begin here
17
4mm pearl beads
17 small beads
10
4mm special large
3mm pearl beads
13
4mm special large
6
pass wire through then pinch wire

⑥ TRUMPET

gold (aqua)
11
small
8
#28 wire 80cm(32")
begin here
14
12 small beads
4mm pearl beads
3mm pearl beads
4mm pearl beads
pass wire through then pinch wire

⑦ VIOLIN

#28 wire 130cm(52")

twist back and finish
begin here
10 small beads
silver (gold)
gold
2×8
3×7
pass through pearl beads, twist twice
4mm pearl beads
10 small beads
3mm pearl beads
gold (white)

THE WIZARD OF OZ CONTINUED FROM PAGE5

CONTINUED FROM PAGE5

⑫ EMERALD CASTLE

wire ① #30 120cm(48")
② #34 20cm(8")

finish
large gold
continue after square beads
clear
green metallic
green
21
15
yellow-green
① begin here
②
light blue
square blue

small
large gold
opaque green
square blue
yellow-green
clear
green
begin here
metallic green
opaque green
wire #30 90cm(36")

⑦~⑪ TOWER

large
small
red
5mm brushed gold pearl bead
metallic green
7
8
9
10
14
12
19th row
connect to 20th row
connect square beads above the 10th row. pass wire through 10th row again
large
small
4mm brushed gold pearl bead
square blue
gold
yellow-green
11
13
15
opaque green
green
begin here
wire #30 150cm(60")
connect square beads above the 8th row. pass wire through the 8th row again
square blue
yellow-green
gold
11
green
begin here
wire #30 100cm(40")

twist together and cut
large
green
3mm gold bugle beads
small clear
4mm jade curved beads
small
5mm brushed gold pearl bead
metallic green
9
13
11
square blue
connect square beads above the 10th row. pass wire through 10th row again
small
twist together and cut
small clear
4mm brushed gold pearl bead
metallic green
gold
8
11
square blue
gold
opaque green
begin here
wire #30 130cm(52")
connect square beads above the 9th row. pass wire through 9th row again
gold
opaque green
10
13
yello-green
begin here
green
wire #30 110cm(44")

54

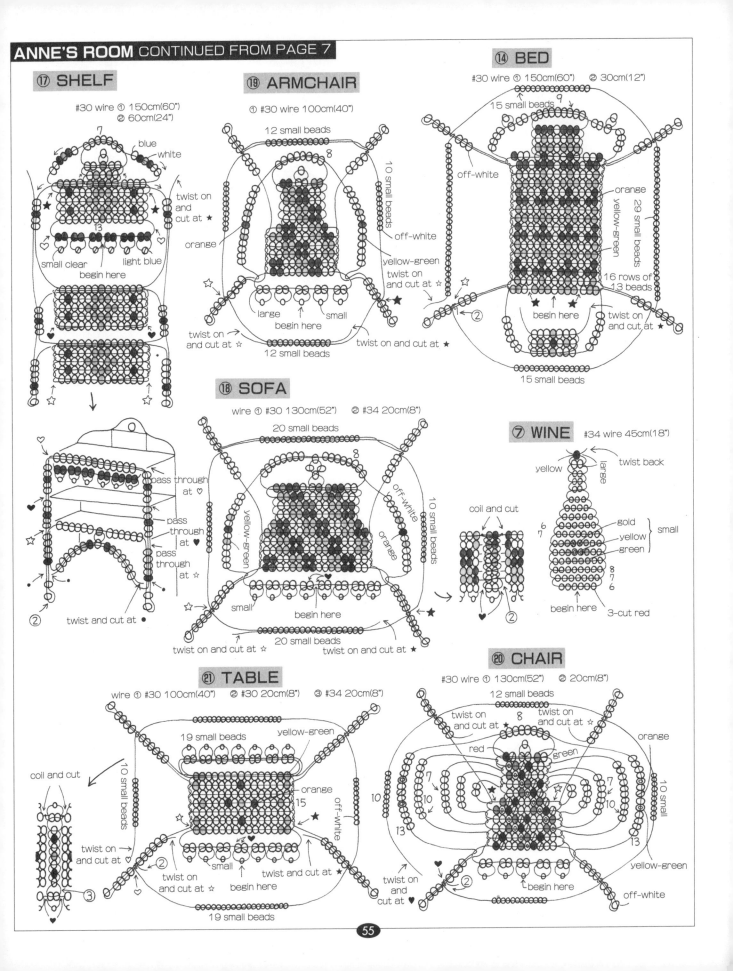

⑰ SHELF

#30 wire ① 150cm(60")
② 60cm(24")

7
blue
white
twist on and cut at ★
13
small clear
light blue
begin here

②
twist and cut at ●

⑲ ARMCHAIR

① #30 wire 100cm(40")

12 small beads
8
10 small beads
off-white
orange
yellow-green
twist on and cut at ☆
large
small
begin here
twist on and cut at ☆
12 small beads
twist on and cut at ★

⑭ BED

#30 wire ① 150cm(60") ② 30cm(12")

15 small beads
9
off-white
orange
yellow-green
29 small beads
16 rows of 13 beads
begin here
twist on and cut at ★
②
15 small beads

⑱ SOFA

wire ① #30 130cm(52") ② #34 20cm(8")

20 small beads
8
off-white
orange
10 small beads
yellow-green
small
begin here
☆
twist on and cut at ☆
twist on and cut at ★
20 small beads

pass through at ♡
pass through at ♥
pass through at ☆

⑦ WINE

#34 wire 45cm(18")

yellow
large
twist back
coil and cut
gold
yellow
green
small
6
7
8
7
6
♥
②
begin here
3-cut red

㉑ TABLE

wire ① #30 100cm(40") ② #30 20cm(8") ③ #34 20cm(8")

19 small beads
yellow-green
10 small beads
coil and cut
orange
15
off-white
twist on and cut at ☆
②
small
♥
twist and cut at ★
twist on and cut at ☆
begin here
③
♥
19 small beads

⑳ CHAIR

#30 wire ① 130cm(52") ② 20cm(8")

12 small beads
twist on and cut at ★
8
twist on and cut at ☆
orange
red
green
7
10
10
7
10
13
10
13
begin here
②
twist on and cut at ♥
yellow-green
off-white

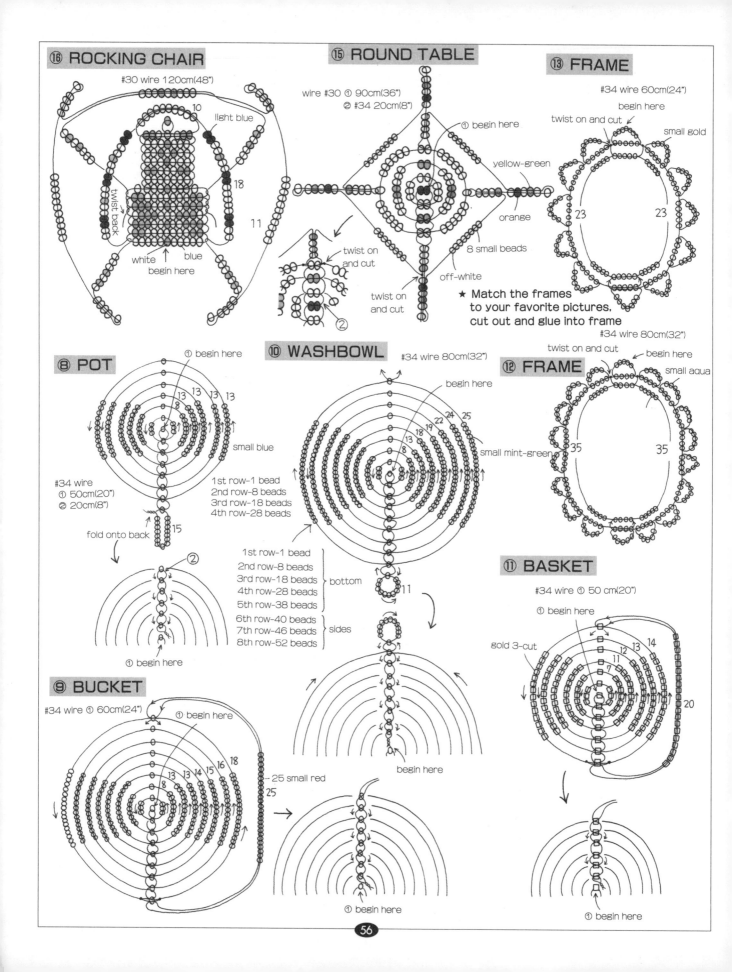

⑯ ROCKING CHAIR

#30 wire 120cm(48")

light blue

10

18

11

twist back

white   blue

begin here

⑮ ROUND TABLE

wire #30 ① 90cm(36")
② #34 20cm(8")

① begin here

yellow-green

orange

8 small beads

off-white

twist on and cut

twist on and cut

②

★ Match the frames
to your favorite pictures,
cut out and glue into frame

⑬ FRAME

#34 wire 60cm(24")

begin here

twist on and cut

small gold

23   23

⑧ POT

① begin here

13 13 13 13

8

small blue

#34 wire
① 50cm(20")
② 20cm(8")

fold onto back

15

②

① begin here

1st row–1 bead
2nd row–8 beads
3rd row–18 beads
4th row–28 beads

⑩ WASHBOWL

#34 wire 80cm(32")

begin here

22 24 25
19
18
13
8

small mint-green

1st row–1 bead
2nd row–8 beads
3rd row–18 beads   bottom
4th row–28 beads
5th row–38 beads

6th row–40 beads
7th row–46 beads   sides
8th row–52 beads

11

begin here

① begin here

⑫ FRAME

#34 wire 80cm(32")

twist on and cut

begin here

small aqua

35   35

⑪ BASKET

#34 wire ① 50 cm(20")

① begin here

gold 3-cut

12 13 14

11

7

20

⑨ BUCKET

#34 wire ① 60cm(24")

① begin here

13 13 14 15 16 18
8

25 small red

25

① begin here

① begin here

56

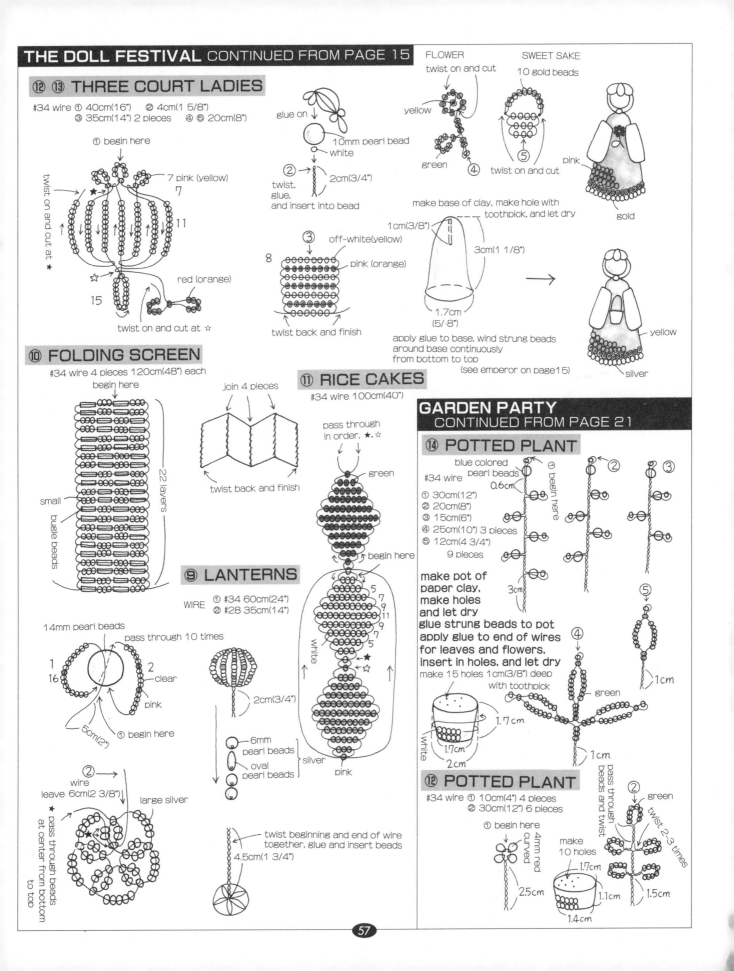

⑫ ⑬ THREE COURT LADIES

#34 wire ① 40cm(16") ② 4cm(1 5/8")
③ 35cm(14") 2 pieces ④ ⑤ 20cm(8")

① begin here

twist on and cut at ★

7 pink (yellow)
7
11
15
red (orange)

twist on and cut at ☆

FLOWER
twist on and cut

yellow

green

④

glue on

10mm pearl bead
white

② twist, glue, and insert into bead

2cm(3/4")

③ off-white(yellow)
8
pink (orange)

twist back and finish

SWEET SAKE
10 gold beads

⑤ twist on and cut

pink

gold

make base of clay, make hole with toothpick, and let dry
1cm(3/8")
3cm(1 1/8")
1.7cm (5/·8")

apply glue to base, wind strung beads around base continuously from bottom to top
(see emperor on page15)

yellow

silver

⑩ FOLDING SCREEN

#34 wire 4 pieces 120cm(48") each
begin here

22 layers

small bugle beads

join 4 pieces

twist back and finish

⑪ RICE CAKES

#34 wire 100cm(40")

pass through in order. ★, ☆

green

begin here

5
7
11
9
7
5
← ★
← ☆

white

silver

pink

⑨ LANTERNS

WIRE ① #34 60cm(24")
② #28 35cm(14")

14mm pearl beads
pass through 10 times
1
16
2 clear
pink
5cm(2")
① begin here

② wire leave 6cm(2 3/8")
large silver
★ pass through beads at center from bottom to top

6mm pearl beads
oval pearl beads

twist beginning and end of wire together, glue and insert beads
4.5cm(1 3/4")

⑭ POTTED PLANT

blue colored pearl beads
0.6cm
#34 wire
① 30cm(12")
② 20cm(8")
③ 15cm(6")
④ 25cm(10") 3 pieces
⑤ 12cm(4 3/4") 9 pieces

① begin here
② ③
3cm
⑤
1cm
④
green

make pot of paper clay, make holes and let dry
glue strung beads to pot
apply glue to end of wires for leaves and flowers, insert in holes, and let dry
make 15 holes 1cm(3/8") deep with toothpick

white
1.7cm
1.7cm
2cm
1cm

⑫ POTTED PLANT

#34 wire ① 10cm(4") 4 pieces
② 30cm(12") 6 pieces

① begin here
4mm red curved
2.5cm

make 10 holes

② green
twist 2-3 times
pass through beads and twist
1.7cm
1.1cm
1.5cm
1.4cm

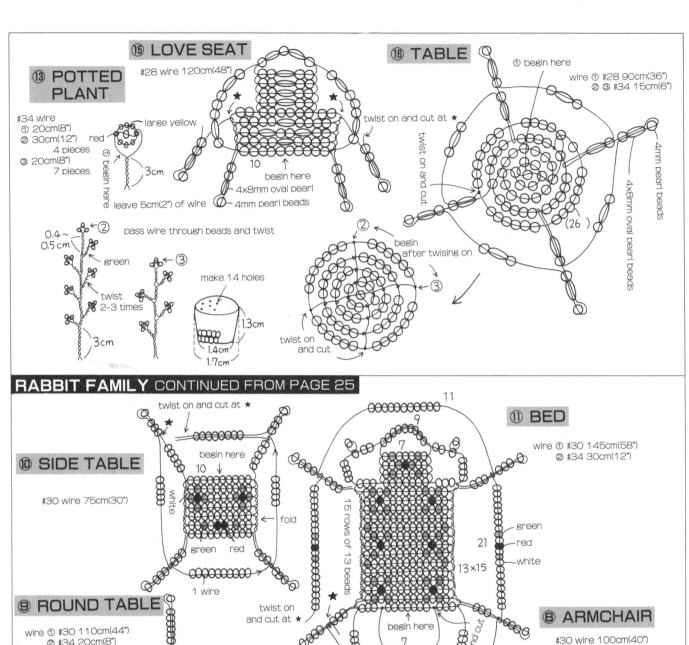

⑬ POTTED PLANT

#34 wire
① 20cm(8")
② 30cm(12")
 4 pieces
③ 20cm(8")
 7 pieces

large yellow
red
3cm
① begin here

leave 5cm(2") of wire

0.4~
0.5cm
②
pass wire through beads and twist
green
③
twist
2-3 times
3cm

make 14 holes
1.3cm
1.4cm
1.7cm

⑮ LOVE SEAT

#28 wire 120cm(48")

twist on and cut at ★
10
begin here
4x8mm oval pearl
4mm pearl beads

⑯ TABLE

① begin here
wire ① #28 90cm(36")
 ② ③ #34 15cm(6")

twist on and cut
twist on and cut
4mm pearl beads
4x8mm oval pearl beads
(26)

②
begin after twising on
③
twist on and cut

RABBIT FAMILY CONTINUED FROM PAGE 25

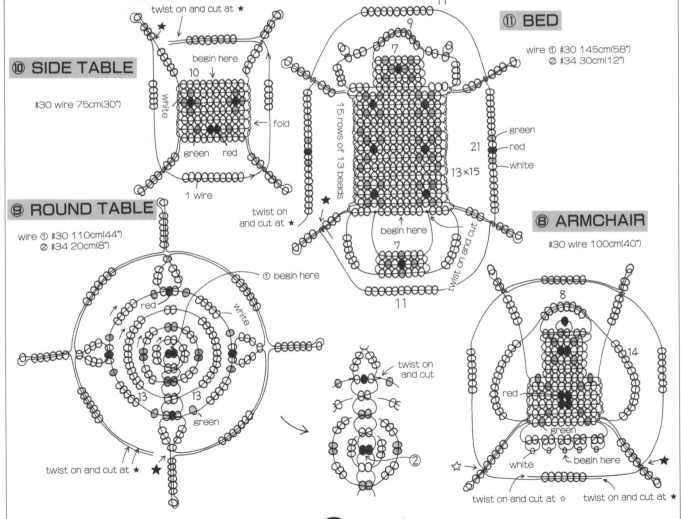

twist on and cut at ★

⑩ SIDE TABLE

#30 wire 75cm(30")

begin here
10
white
fold
green   red
green
1 wire

⑪ BED

wire ① #30 145cm(58")
 ② #34 30cm(12")

11
9
7
15 rows of 13 beads
green
red
white
21
13×15
begin here
twist on and cut
7
11

⑨ ROUND TABLE

wire ① #30 110cm(44")
 ② #34 20cm(8")

① begin here
red
white
13   13
green
twist on and cut at ★ ★

twist on and cut
②

⑧ ARMCHAIR

#30 wire 100cm(40")

8
14
red
green
begin here
white
twist on and cut at ☆   twist on and cut at ★

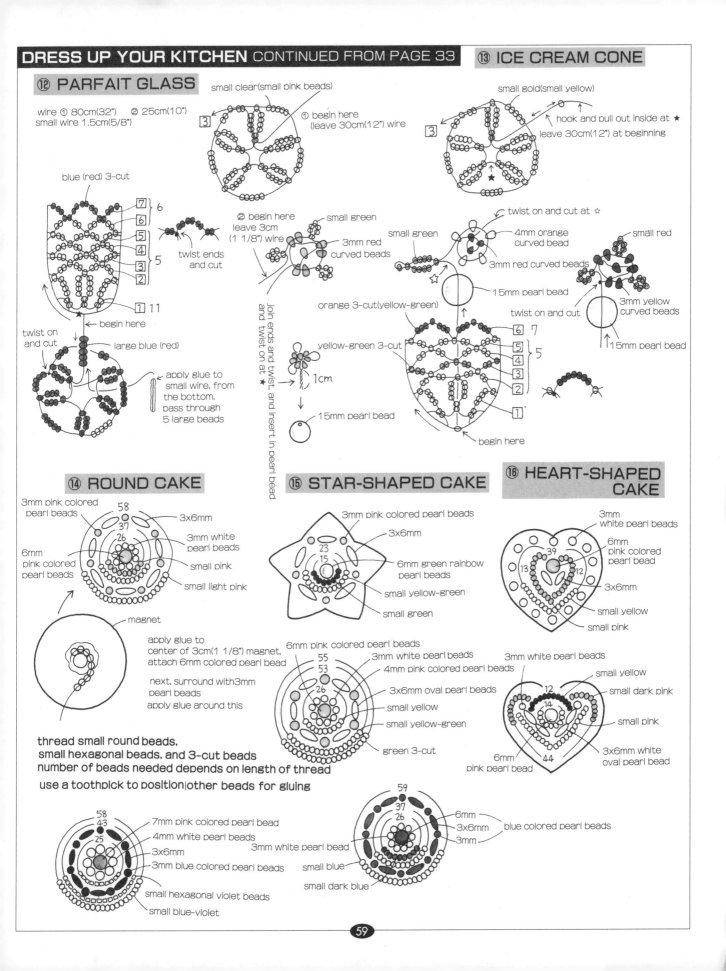

⑫ PARFAIT GLASS

wire ① 80cm(32") ② 25cm(10")
small wire 1.5cm(5/8")

small clear(small pink beads)

① begin here
(leave 30cm(12") wire

blue (red) 3-cut

⑦ 6
⑥
⑤
④ 5
③
②
① 11

twist ends and cut

twist on and cut

begin here

large blue (red)

twist on and cut

apply glue to small wire, from the bottom, pass through 5 large beads

② begin here leave 3cm (1 1/8") wire

small green

3mm red curved beads

orange 3-cut(yellow-green)

yellow-green 3-cut

Join ends and twist, and twist on at ★ and insert in pearl bead

1cm

15mm pearl bead

⑬ ICE CREAM CONE

small gold(small yellow)

hook and pull out inside at ★
leave 30cm(12") at beginning

small green

twist on and cut at ☆

4mm orange curved bead

small red

3mm red curved beads

15mm pearl bead

twist on and cut

3mm yellow curved beads

15mm pearl bead

⑥ 7
⑤
④ 5
③
②
①

begin here

⑭ ROUND CAKE

3mm pink colored pearl beads

58
37
26

3x6mm

3mm white pearl beads

6mm pink colored pearl beads

small pink

small light pink

magnet

apply glue to center of 3cm(1 1/8") magnet. attach 6mm colored pearl bead

next, surround with 3mm pearl beads
apply glue around this

thread small round beads, small hexagonal beads, and 3-cut beads
number of beads needed depends on length of thread

use a toothpick to position other beads for gluing

58
43
25

7mm pink colored pearl bead
4mm white pearl beads
3x6mm
3mm blue colored pearl beads
small hexagonal violet beads
small blue-violet

⑮ STAR-SHAPED CAKE

3mm pink colored pearl beads

3x6mm

23
15

6mm green rainbow pearl beads

small yellow-green

small green

6mm pink colored pearl beads
3mm white pearl beads
4mm pink colored pearl beads

55
53
26

3x6mm oval pearl beads

small yellow

small yellow-green

green 3-cut

59
37
26

6mm
3x6mm
3mm

blue colored pearl beads

3mm white pearl bead

small blue

small dark blue

⑯ HEART-SHAPED CAKE

3mm white pearl beads

6mm pink colored pearl bead

39

13
12

3x6mm

small yellow

small pink

3mm white pearl beads

small yellow

12

small dark pink

14

small pink

6mm pink pearl bead

44

3x6mm white oval pearl bead

SUMMER AT THE BEACH CONTINUED FROM PAGE 35

⑨ SHOULDER BAG

#34 wire ① 60cm(24") ② 55cm(22") ③ 25cm(10") ④ 15cm(6")

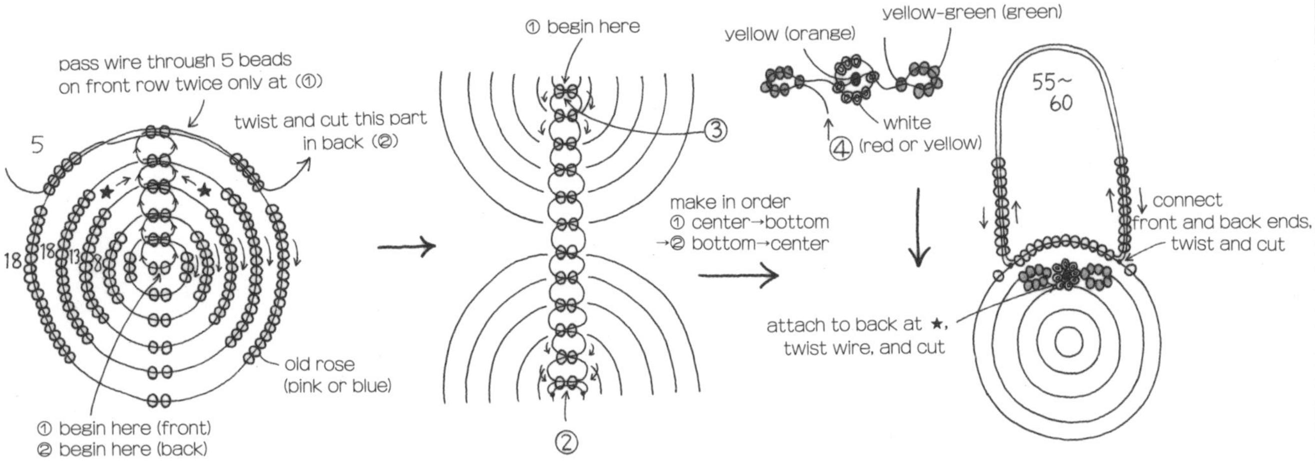

pass wire through 5 beads
on front row twice only at (①)
twist and cut this part
in back (②)
5
18
18
13
old rose
(pink or blue)
① begin here (front)
② begin here (back)
① begin here
③
②
make in order
① center→bottom
→② bottom→center
yellow (orange)
yellow-green (green)
white
④ (red or yellow)
55~
60
connect
front and back ends,
twist and cut
attach to back at ★,
twist wire, and cut

⑧ HAT

#34 wire ① 90cm(36") ② 30cm(12")

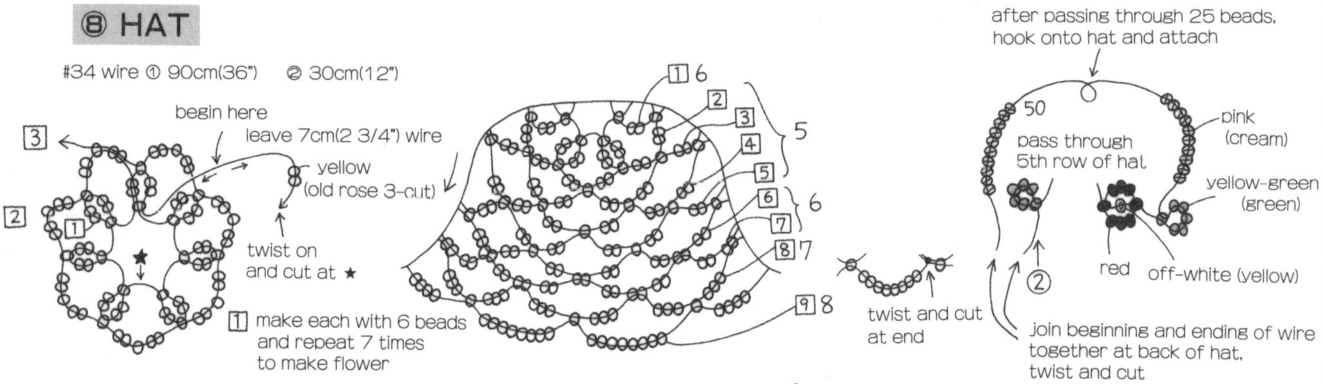

begin here
leave 7cm(2 3/4") wire
yellow
(old rose 3-cut)
3
2
1
twist on
and cut at ★
1 make each with 6 beads
and repeat 7 times
to make flower
1 6
2
3
4
5
6
7
8 7
9 8
5
6
twist and cut
at end
after passing through 25 beads,
hook onto hat and attach
50
pass through
5th row of hat
pink
(cream)
yellow-green
(green)
red
off-white (yellow)
②
join beginning and ending of wire
together at back of hat,
twist and cut

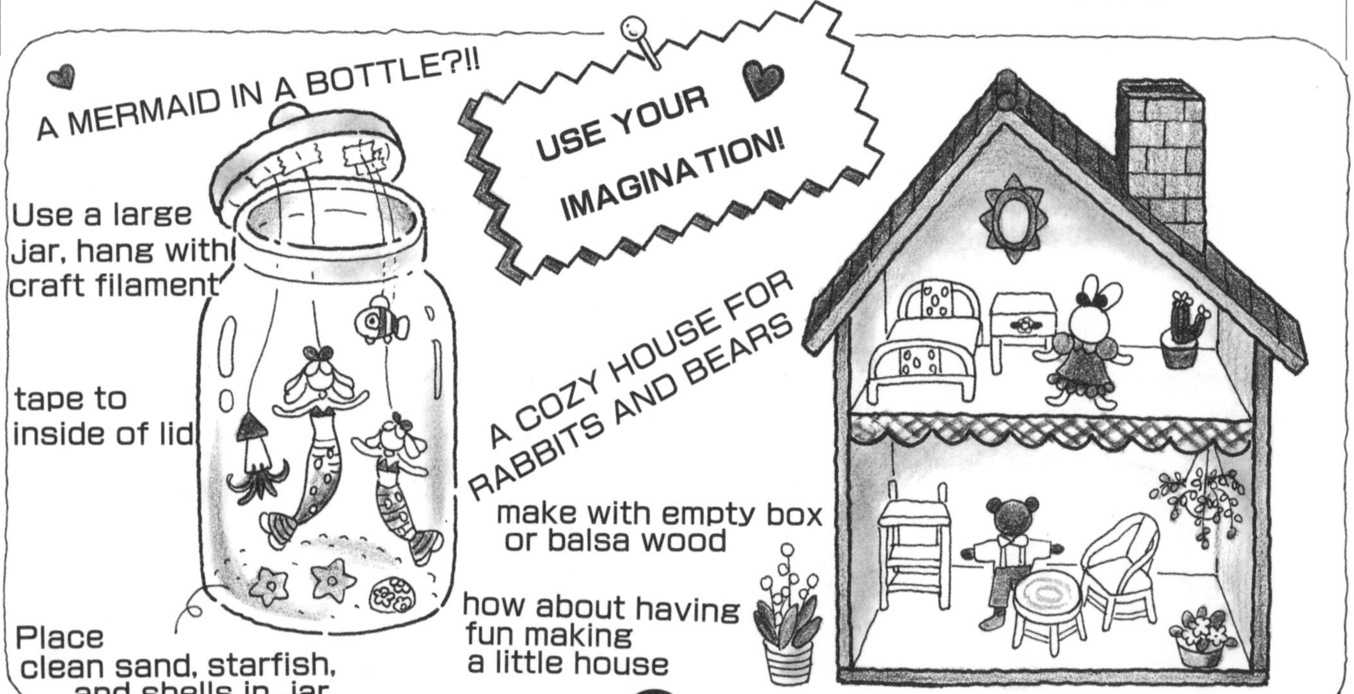

A MERMAID IN A BOTTLE?!!
USE YOUR
IMAGINATION!
Use a large
jar, hang with
craft filament
tape to
inside of lid
Place
clean sand, starfish,
and shells in jar
A COZY HOUSE FOR
RABBITS AND BEARS
make with empty box
or balsa wood
how about having
fun making
a little house

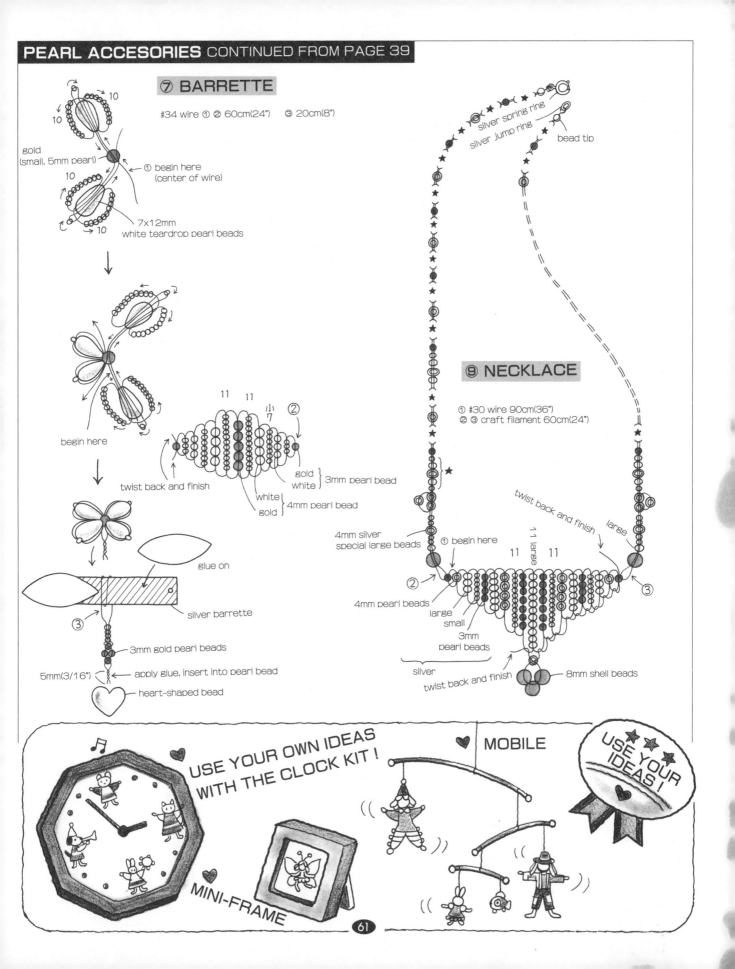

⑦ BARRETTE

#34 wire ① ② 60cm(24")   ③ 20cm(8")

10
10
10

gold
(small, 5mm pearl)

① begin here
(center of wire)

10

7x12mm
white teardrop pearl beads

begin here

11   11
②

twist back and finish

gold
white } 3mm pearl bead

white
gold } 4mm pearl bead

glue on

③

silver barrette

3mm gold pearl beads

5mm(3/16") ← apply glue, insert into pearl bead

heart-shaped bead

⑨ NECKLACE

① #30 wire 90cm(36")
② ③ craft filament 60cm(24")

silver spring ring
silver jump ring
bead tip

twist back and finish   large

4mm silver
special large beads

① begin here

②

11 large   11

4mm pearl beads

large
small
3mm
pearl beads

③

silver

twist back and finish

8mm shell beads

USE YOUR OWN IDEAS
WITH THE CLOCK KIT !

♥ MOBILE

USE YOUR
IDEAS !

MINI-FRAME

⑨ BROOCH

#34 wire 60cm(24")

make same as barrette

small silver beads

8 8

6x10mm white
teardrop pearl beads

4mm gold pearl beads

3mm gold pearl beads

gold shower pin

⑥ NECKLACE

nylon thread 320cm(126")

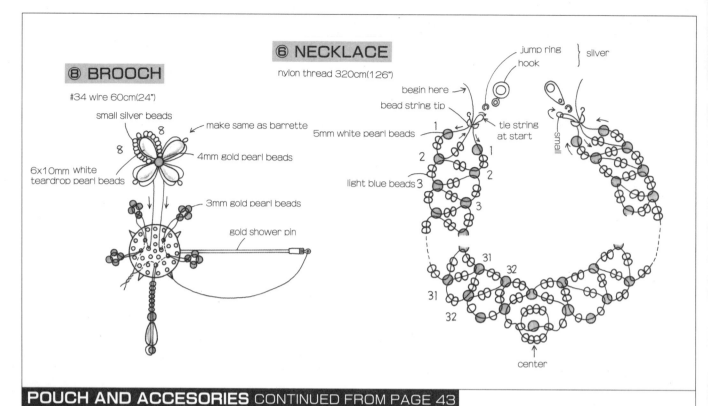

jump ring
hook

silver

begin here

bead string tip

5mm white pearl beads

tie string
at start

small

light blue beads

1 2 3

31 32

center

POUCH AND ACCESORIES CONTINUED FROM PAGE 43

⑩ BARRETTE

#34 wire ① 80cm(32") 2 pieces
② 80cm(32")

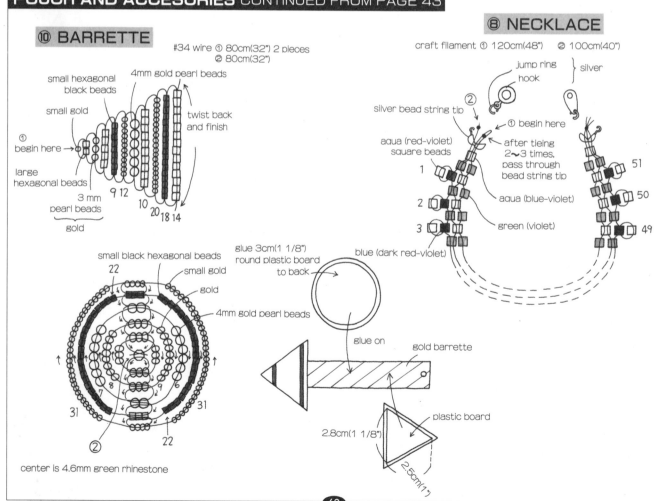

small hexagonal
black beads

small gold

4mm gold pearl beads

twist back
and finish

① begin here →

large
hexagonal beads

3 mm
pearl beads

gold

9 12   10   20 18 14

small black hexagonal beads

22

small gold

gold

4mm gold pearl beads

8 7 6

31 31

② 22

center is 4.6mm green rhinestone

glue 3cm(1 1/8")
round plastic board
to back

blue (dark red-violet)

glue on

gold barrette

plastic board

2.8cm(1 1/8")

2.5cm(1")

⑧ NECKLACE

craft filament ① 120cm(48") ② 100cm(40")

jump ring
hook

silver

silver bead string tip

② ① begin here

aqua (red-violet)
square beads

after tieing
2~3 times,
pass through
bead string tip

aqua (blue-violet)

green (violet)

1 2 3

51 50 49

62

⑨ BARRETTE

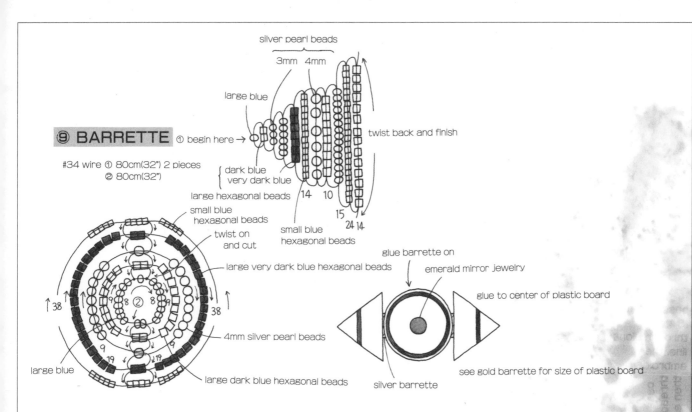

#34 wire ① 80cm(32") 2 pieces
② 80cm(32")

silver pearl beads
3mm 4mm

large blue

twist back and finish

dark blue
very dark blue

large hexagonal beads

14 10

15

24 14

small blue
hexagonal beads

twist on
and cut

large very dark blue hexagonal beads

large blue

4mm silver pearl beads

large dark blue hexagonal beads

small blue
hexagonal beads

glue barrette on

emerald mirror jewelry

glue to center of plastic board

see gold barrette for size of plastic board

silver barrette

⑦ CAT POUCH

MATERIALS (ALL SILVER, UNLESS OTHERWISE INDICATED)

50x50cm(20x20") black velvet
black felt 20x20cm(8x8") 2 pieces
large round beads
large triangular beads
59 6mm sequins
19 5mm sequins

3 5x10mm design rhinestones
3 4.6mm rhinestones
2 8.4mm rhinestones
6mm thick cord 100cm(40")
#34 wire 70cm(28")
snap or magnetic clasp

see page 16 for embroidery instructions

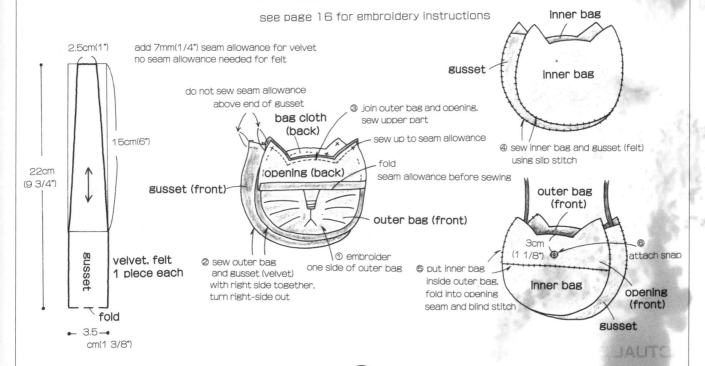

2.5cm(1")

add 7mm(1/4") seam allowance for velvet
no seam allowance needed for felt

22cm
(9 3/4")

15cm(6")

velvet, felt
1 piece each

gusset

fold

3.5
cm(1 3/8")

do not sew seam allowance
above end of gusset

bag cloth
(back)

gusset (front)

opening (back)

② sew outer bag
and gusset (velvet)
with right side together,
turn right-side out

③ join outer bag and opening,
sew upper part

sew up to seam allowance

fold
seam allowance before sewing

outer bag (front)

① embroider
one side of outer bag

inner bag

gusset

inner bag

④ sew inner bag and gusset (felt)
using slip stitch

outer bag
(front)

3cm
(1 1/8")

⑥
attach snap

⑤ put inner bag
inside outer bag,
fold into opening
seam and blind stitch

inner bag

opening
(front)

gusset

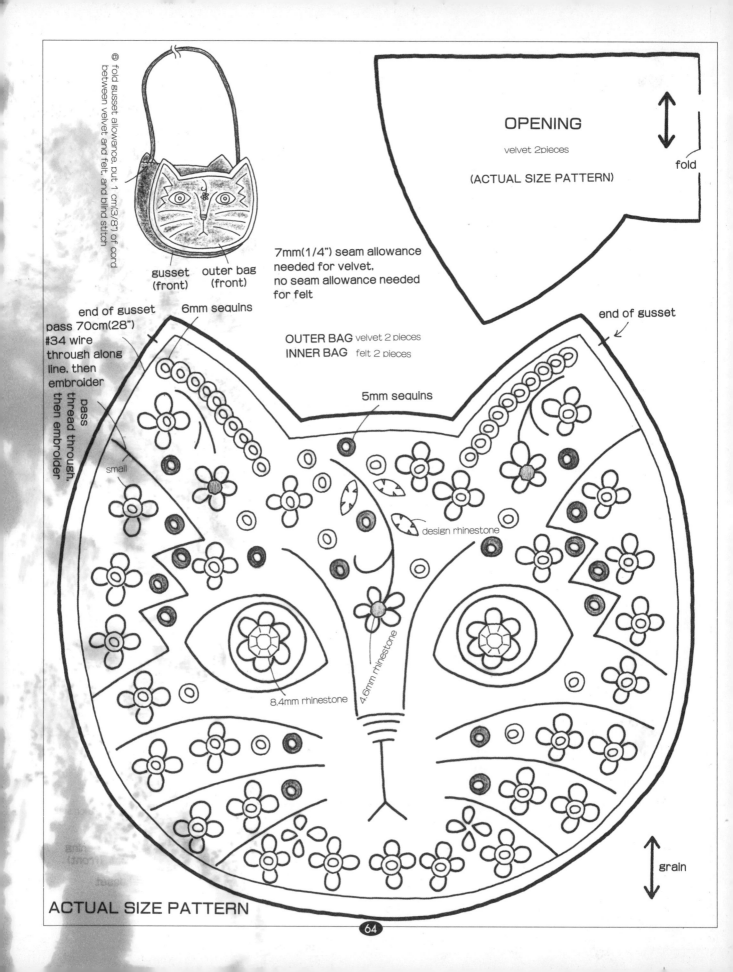

© fold gusset allowance, put 1 cm(3/8") of cord between velvet and felt, and blind stitch

gusset (front)   outer bag (front)

OPENING

velvet 2pieces

(ACTUAL SIZE PATTERN)

fold

7mm(1/4") seam allowance needed for velvet, no seam allowance needed for felt

OUTER BAG velvet 2 pieces
INNER BAG felt 2 pieces

end of gusset
pass 70cm(28") #34 wire through along line, then embroider

pass thread through, then embroider

small

6mm sequins

end of gusset

5mm sequins

design rhinestone

4.6mm rhinestone

8.4mm rhinestone

grain

ACTUAL SIZE PATTERN